SPACE COLONY ™

OFFICIAL STRATEGY GUIDE

By Rick Barba

CONTENTS

GATHERING

CHAPTER 1: GETTING STARTED

Welcome to the official strategy guide for *Space Colony*, the fabulous (and funny) new "people-sim world-builder in space" from Firefly Studios. Without further ado, let's take a look at what this book has to offer you.

HOW TO MASTER *SPACE COLONY*

This guide focuses on the two infallible paths to success in *Space Colony*. Here's a quick breakdown of the knowledge you need for game mastery, and how this book provides that knowledge.

Know Your Colonists

First and foremost, you must understand *thoroughly* the needs and desires of your 20 colonists. And when we say "thoroughly," we mean "in statistical detail." That's what you get in spades in our **Chapter 2: Character Profiles**.

Our descriptions and stats tables (provided by Firefly Studios and generously collated by Gathering producer, Tim Beggs) reveal the exact nature of each colonist's unique set of needs—how strong each need is, and how often it must be satisfied. You also learn *who* and *what* each colonist likes and dislikes. This knowledge is crucial for successful management of a colony.

Play the Campaign

Secondly, you must learn how to be more efficient in the fundamental aspects of *Space Colony* gameplay—from laying out your colony base to economic development (mining, industry, tourism) to military tactics versus alien incursion. This is exactly what our detailed, step-by-step walkthroughs of the game's 24 campaign missions are designed to teach you.

Firefly Studios designed these missions to progress seamlessly from introductory to advanced game mechanics. Our walkthroughs in **Chapter 3: The Catherwood Missions** give you efficient base-building techniques and worker management tactics. We also introduce you to the basic mechanics of colony mining and industrial activity.

Chapter 4: Civilian Path provides a more advanced education in economic development, with an expanded look at colony industry and tourism. In particular, you learn how to transform a bleak, forbidding planet into a 10-star tourist attraction.

And finally, **Chapter 5: Military Path** gives you the strategies you need to survive fast-paced combat against hostile aliens. By the time you finish playing through these missions under our guidance, you'll be able to deal with *anything* slimy or spiky or just plain disgusting.

Take a peek at our **Appendix: Romance Stats**, too. It has some interesting information on the romantic possibilities of colony life.

How to Cheat

Get on the Internet and go to gaming sites with cheat codes—a good one is Gameguru Mania at *www.ggmania.com*. Then check out the listings for *Space Colony*. In this case, Gameguru Mania provides small programs for download called "trainers" that you can access while playing the game. These are *very* sneaky and wonderful, if you're stuck and impatient.

Trainers actually program certain keystrokes in the game to become cheat hotkeys. For example, one *Space Colony* trainer reprograms the [F1] key to provide infinite credits and sets [F2] to return the game to normal. Another trainer available at the Gameguru Mania site sets [F2] to boost your credit balance, [F3] to provide infinite power, and [F4] to provide infinite oxygen.

CHAPTER 2
CHARACTER PROFILES

Here it is, folks—the chapter where you really get your money's worth. *Space Colony* is primarily about your 20 colonists—their needs and motivations, skills and idiosyncrasies, likes and dislikes, and of course their relationships to each other. Intimate knowledge of these things gives you the power to take much better care of your people. And that means they work harder for you.

So if you can get a handle on the psychology of each one of your *Space Colony* characters, you're well on your way to mastery of this game.

Some of this chapter is review info, but most of it reveals new and privileged information—the super-secret numbers that underlie *Space Colony* behavior patterns. So read on for a statistical glimpse into the deepest needs and desires of all 20 colonists, person by person. We'll show you *exactly* what things they like and dislike, and how much.

2-1. It's all about character in Space Colony.

HAPPINESS: THE SEVEN BASIC NEEDS

Each operative in *Space Colony* has seven basic needs—Financial, Entertainment, Human Contact, Food, Sleep, Hygiene, and Health. The state of each need (high or low) is measured in a corresponding colored bar on the Colonist Panel. When combined, these seven needs determine the colonist's overall Happiness (as measured in the Happiness bar). And overall Happiness determines the colonist's willingness to work.

Sections 3.4 to 3.6 of the *Space Colony* game manual provide an excellent overview of the Colonist Panel and these needs, but we'll add a few notes here before we get to our in-depth profiles of each colonist.

The Needs "Pulse"

All Need bars sink lower over time. The bars drop in small "pulses" that occur at regularly timed intervals. These intervals are measured in units of time called "game ticks," and they differ from need to need and from colonist to colonist.

For comparison, 200 game ticks is about 30 seconds, 400 game ticks is 60 seconds, and so on. These aren't locked intervals, however. Pulse can be affected by other factors—for example, the Hygiene pulse interval changes if base litter is high or low.

For example, Candy's Sleep Need drops in a "pulse" every 200 game ticks, which is normal. But her Human Contact Need drops four times as fast, pulsing downward every 50 ticks. In contrast, Mr. Zhang's Human Contact Need is steady, pulsing every 200 ticks. But his Sleep Need plummets downward at a pulse every 25 ticks! Clearly, the man needs his naps, big time.

The pulse intervals for all needs are listed for each colonist in our character profiles. As you can see, these tables will give you some valuable insight into who needs what, and how often.

Special Needs: How They Affect Happiness

Some people have *special* needs. Hoshi and Kita have a gnawing need to be entertained; Tami desperately needs gabby Human Contact; Dean is fastidious about his Personal Hygiene. Special needs, indicated by a star next to the corresponding need icon on the Colonist Panel (see 2-2), affect a colonist's overall Happiness more than other needs do.

Make sure special needs are met so the colonist's overall Happiness bar doesn't go down too fast. For example, Stig has the special need for Food. If he gets dirty and his Hygiene Need bar drops into the red zone, his overall Happiness bar drops somewhat, but hardly tanks. However, if Stig gets *hungry*—that is, his starred Food bar drops into the red zone—then his overall Happiness bar drops much more dramatically.

2-2. Stig has a special need for Food, indicated by the star next to the Food icon on his Colonist Panel. Special needs affect overall Happiness more than other needs do.

The good news is that satisfying a colonist's special need makes his or her overall Happiness rating go up faster, as well. Stig gets a bigger overall Happiness boost from eating than Venus or Charles.

Entertainment: The Custom Need

Again, each *Space Colony* character has a specific set of needs. Food, Sleep, and Hygiene are very straightforward; it's easy to figure out how to satisfy them. If a colonist is hungry, you send him to the Mess Hall or Restaurant. If she's tired, send her to bed. The specific activity designed to satisfy a need like Food or Hygiene is pretty easy to discern.

Then there's Entertainment.

This need is only "basic" in that everyone needs to be entertained. Other than that, it can be a tricky one to figure out. Entertainment preferences are quite different from person to person in *Space Colony*. Colonists may find very different activities to be enjoyable—for example, Dean loves working out, yet Tami despises exercise and very much prefers to booze it up in the nearest Bar.

Thus, Entertainment is the most individualized need in *Space Colony*—and, therefore, the most difficult one to manage efficiently. You have to really *know* your people's likes and dislikes. Both Venus' Description and the Psychiatrist's Report on each colonist (found in the game and in the game manual, section 3.0) are good places to start. But in the following character profiles, the Entertainment tables will take your knowledge several layers deeper.

How the Entertainment Tables Measure Satisfaction

Each character profile in this section includes a table listing all facilities related to the Entertainment needs of *Space Colony* operatives—Bar, Disco, Meditation Room, Slot Machine, and so on. In the table, each facility has a number rating. This number indicates exactly how fast (if at all) the facility raises (or lowers) that character's Entertainment bar when used.

Here are some things to remember when perusing the Entertainment tables:

- All ratings are on a 20-point scale, from −10 up to 10.
- A *positive number* (1 up to 10) means that when the character uses that facility, his/her Entertainment Need bar rises. The higher the positive number, the faster the Entertainment bar rises.
- A *negative number* (-1 down to -10) means that the character's Entertainment bar actually *lowers* when he/she uses that facility. The lower the negative number, the faster the Entertainment bar drops.
- Zero (0) is neutral—that is, the activity does not affect the colonist's Entertainment rating at all. The bar doesn't move up or down.

For example, Tami hates exercise—indeed, with a value of -8, she deeply *loathes* exercise. So if you direct Tami to use any exercise equipment, her Entertainment Need bar drops considerably.

On the other hand, both Dean and Nailer *like* to exercise; however, Dean (at 9) likes to exercise more than Nailer does (at 5). Both fellows get a boost in their Entertainment Need bar when they use exercise equipment, but Dean gets a *faster* boost than Nailer.

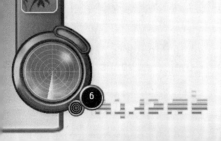

HAPPINESS AND WORK

Thriving space colonies are packed with happy, hardworking people. These two qualities—*happy* and *hardworking*—are intimately intertwined. The most important thing to remember when assigning jobs and developing your *Space Colony* economy is this: the better you satisfy your colonists' needs, the happier your people are, and the longer (and thus harder) they work.

The Shift Clock

The relationship between *happy* and *hardworking* is clearly displayed in each colonist's Shift Clock. The Shift Clock appears to the right of the Needs and Desires bars (see 2-3) in the Colonist Panel that appears when you click on a colonist (or click on the colonist's head icon in the lower-right corner).

2-3. Each Colonist has a Shift Clock that displays his/her division of work and relaxation hours. The happier your worker, the less time they need off the job.

The highlighted part of the Shift Clock—that is, the part outlined by a color—looks like a pie chart. It indicates the hours this colonist freely chooses to work. The missing slice of the pie indicates the hours when the colonist prefers to relax and will not work, unless so ordered. The moving clock hand indicates where the colonist is at in his/her cycle of work and relaxation.

> Note that the clock's highlight color matches the current color of the Overall Happiness bar—red for low happiness, yellow for medium happiness, or green for high happiness.

"SPECIAL FRIENDS": HOW COLONISTS FALL IN LOVE

When you select one colonist (let's say Dean) and then click on a second colonist (let's say Candy), a social interaction menu appears over Candy's head (see 2-4). Dean has three interaction choices: Friendship (only if there's a Social Area in your base), Small Talk, or Romance.

Small Talk: Dean and Candy stop and chat for a few seconds. This fully satisfies each person's Human Contact need, but has no effect on the personal relationship rating between the two.

Friendship: Dean and Candy find the nearest Social Area (a pair of chairs) and talk. This fully satisfies each person's Human Contact need. It also raises the personal relationship rating between Dean and Candy.

Romance: This brings up the Romance menu, a series of icons that represent date types that Dean can propose to Candy. When you move the cursor over each icon, you can see one of these options—for example, "Want to get a drink?" The percent listed underneath the question indicates the chance that Candy will answer yes to Dean's proposal.

If Candy agrees to any type of date (Drink, Dancing, Jacuzzi, etc.), the icon for that date is filled with a big green checkmark. When checked, that type of date is no longer available for Dean to propose to Candy. Subsequent date proposals from Dean to Candy will have to be of another type.

2-4. The Romance selection from the social interaction menu brings up a series of date proposals. Each successful date fills in one heart in the "Will you be mine?" icon. Each filled heart increases the odds of a "Yes" answer to "Will you be mine?"

The last and biggest Romance icon is "Will you be mine?" Note the three small heart icons on its perimeter (see 2-4). Each time Candy answers "Yes" to a date proposal from Dean, one of those heart icons gets filled in. Each filled-in heart increases the chance that Candy will answer "Yes" to "Will you be mine?" You can see the percentage of that chance of success under the question when you move the cursor over the "Will you be mine?" icon.

Even if all three heart icons are filled in, there is always a chance (sometimes big, depending on who's asking whom) that the respondent will answer "No" to the question "Will you be mine?" If that happens, one of the filled hearts becomes unfilled, and the type of the couple's last date becomes unchecked in the Romance menu the next time Dean asks Candy on a date.

So rejection lowers the odds of acceptance the next time Dean asks, "Will you be mine?" To regain the best chance of success, Dean should ask Candy on another date to refill the now-unfilled heart.

Got it? Whew!

But wait. There's one other bit of complication. The Romance menu only advances in one direction. If Candy turns around and proposes a date to Dean, she starts with a clean, unchecked Romance menu and three unfilled hearts on the "Will you be mine?" icon. So even if she's accepted three date proposals from Dean, she starts with a clean slate if she decides to ask *him* on a date.

To review tables covering the odds that each character will answer "Yes" to other *Space Colony* characters in each of the Romance/date questions, see *Appendix A: Romance Tables*.

COLONIST PROFILES

Finally! Time to meet your *Space Colony* team, up close and personal. The following profiles provide an intimate, statistical look at all 20 primary operatives in the game. Before we start the alphabetical roll call, note that we've alphabetized according to first names. That's the way the game recognizes your operatives, so we'll follow suit.

Fast Facts

Age:	28
Home:	England
Likes:	Exercise, Combat, Thrills
Special Needs:	Health
Special Skills (Star Rating):	Nutrient Extraction (1)
Basic Skills:	Mining, Weeding, Power, Oxygen, Cleaning, Maintenance
Walking Speed:	Fast

Profile: Ashia

Ashia Green, athletic and hip, hails from South London. She's an upbeat person, and Venus is quite fond of her personality and work ethic.

Basic/Special Needs

A former athlete waylaid by injury, Ashia is a workout fanatic. Unable to stand still when not walking, she hops off a few quick jumping jacks until it's time to move on to the next task. This love of fitness means Ashia isn't as picky about Hygiene as some colonists, but she does need to replenish those burned-up calories with more frequent meals.

Ashia's high-octane personality gives her a craving for extra entertainment and social contact, too. And Health is a special concern. From time to time she needs a quick trip to the nearest Medi Bay to rehab her old injury.

Entertainment

With Ashia, it's all about fitness. Nothing else comes close. A stint on the Running Machine or Stairclimber will boost her spirits (and Entertainment bar) with amazing alacrity.

Sure, she enjoys an occasional session in the Combat Arena or on the Golf course, and she likes to burn off energy in the pursuit of thrill (Virtuality Chair or Zero Gravity Playroom) or dancing in the Disco. But when Ashia really needs a strong dose of Entertainment, send her *directly* to the nearest exercise machine.

2-5. Ashia's favorite activity is working out on any one of the exercise machines.

Other Notable Attributes

A moderately intelligent girl, Ashia can learn new skills fairly easily. She's an easygoing sort, so she has very high tolerance for both noise and rubbish. If the rigors of colony life manage to drive her nuts, Ashia responds extremely well to counseling—much faster than she does to detention.

Relationships

Ashia's favorite colonist is Venus, by far, but she's also fond of Bhoomi, Billy Bob, and Dean. These four can never become Ashia's enemies. On the other hand, she has to work awfully hard to tolerate Greg, Barbara, and especially Babette.

Taking Ashia's Pulse

The following table shows how quickly Ashia's six specific Need bars drop. The numbers measure how many units of game-time pass between each "pulse." A pulse lowers the particular Need bar a fraction. Thus, the lower the number, the faster the bar goes down. A zero (0) means the character has no need in this category.

2-6. You have to work hard to increase Ashia's extremely low initial impression of Babette.

Need Bar for:	Time Between Downward Pulses
Money	200
Entertainment	100
Human Contact	100
Food	100
Hygiene	400
Sleep	200

(Lower number = Need Bar drops faster)

Entertainment Needs

A positive number for an activity means the Entertainment bar moves up. A negative number means the bar moves down. Zero (0) means the bar doesn't move at all in either direction.

ENTERTAINMENT: ASHIA

Activity	Entertainment Satisfaction Provided
Exercise	10
Thrill	2
Combat Arena	2
Bar	0
Luxury Bar	0
Meditation Room	1
Library/Trainer	0
Piano	0
Relaxation Pod	0
Disco	1
Restaurant	0
Sauna	1
Jacuzzi	1
Observatory	0
Viewing Platform	0
Golf	2
Zoo Exhibit	0
Virtual Shop	0
Slot Machine	0

Exercise = Rowing/Running Machines, Stairclimber

Thrill = Virtuality Chair, Zero-Gravity Playroom

Miscellaneous Attributes

Attribute	Rating
Intelligence (0-10)	5
(Higher number = Learns faster at Library or Trainer)	
Chance of Insanity (0-10)	4
(Higher number = Greater chance of going insane)	
Greenery Benefit (0-10)	2
(Higher number = More satisfaction derived from plants)	
Noise Tolerance (0-5)	1
(Higher number = More intolerant)	
Expected Salary (0-6)	3
(Higher number = Values money more)	
Happiness Boost from Pets (0-5)	1
Litter Drop Rate (0-6)	1
(Higher number = Dirtier)	
Rubbish Tolerance (0-5)	1
(Higher number = More intolerant)	
Response to Counseling (1-10)	10

Basic Relationships

The following table lists Ashia's starting relationship with each of the other 19 operatives in *Space Colony*. A positive number means the relationship starts in the Friend range, with the highest possible friendship being 100. A negative number indicates a start in the Enemy range, with the deepest interpersonal loathing at -100.

A relationship cannot drop any further than 50 points from the starting value listed in the table. However, it can rise clear up to 100 if properly nurtured.

ASHIA'S STARTING RELATIONSHIPS

Relationship with:	Rating (-100 to 100)	Relationship with:	Rating (-100 to 100)
Venus	81	Vasilios	31
Stig	12	Hoshi	2
Tami	-13	Kita	3
Slim	-14	Mr. Zhang	34
Dean	65	Greg	-55
Candy	46	Babette	-66
Billy Bob	67	Nailer	17
Nikolai	18	Bhoomi	68
Daisy	49	Barbara	-57
Captain	4		

Babette Devereux

Fast Facts

Age: 19	
Home: France	
Likes: Piano, Luxury Bar, Restaurant	
Dislikes: Golf	
Special Needs: Hygiene, Health	
Special Skills (Star Rating): None	
Basic Skills: Oxygen	
Walking Speed: Slow	
Walking Speed: Fast	

Profile

The Psychiatrist's Reports points out that Babette is known locally as "The Princess." Venus adds: "She gets on my nerves." What more do you need to know? Well, okay, she can work the Oxygen console. Other than that—let's see now, what else can Babette do? Surely there's something.

Nope, she's worthless.

Basic/Special Needs

Babette's one of the few characters with more than one special need. Hygiene and Health are important to her, causing her more overall unhappiness as they drop. And her Hygiene bar drops faster than normal. But Babette's not a total whine queen. All of her other Need bars drop at a normal rate. Just pop her in the shower regularly, and she shouldn't cause any special management problems.

Entertainment

Babette loves playing the piano with a passion that you'd have to be French perhaps to understand. She's also very, very fond of champagne cocktails at the Luxury Bar or fine meals in the Restaurant. If those aren't available, she'll happily browse through the Virtual Shop or take a long, languorous rest in the Relaxation Pod. Disco dancing keeps her amused, as well.

Babette equally and deeply despises Golf and Zoo Exhibits, finding both to be amongst the lowest expressions of human culture. She's also quite averse to exercise of any sort.

2-7. Babette's favorite activity is playing the piano.

2-8. Babette equally despises Golf and Zoo Exhibits.

Other Notable Attributes

Babette has an extremely low tolerance for noise when she's sleeping. She also has the lowest tolerance possible for rubbish in the base. So, okay, maybe she *is* a whine queen. But she's smart enough to make learning or training less than excruciating, so it is possible to teach daddy's little princess some useful skills.

Relationships

Right off the shuttle, Babette starts out on bad terms with no less than half of the 20 colonists. In particular, she locks horns with Ashia and Daisy, and her initial feelings toward Stig and Billy Bob aren't much better. She starts off very good with Candy, however, and she finds both Charles and Bhoomi exceedingly tolerable, too.

Taking Babette's Pulse

Here's a look at how quickly Babette's six specific Need bars drop. The numbers represent how many units of game-time before the next "pulse" occurs for that Need bar. Each pulse lowers Babette's Need bar a fraction. Thus, the lower the number, the faster the bar goes down. A zero (0) means the character has no need in this category.

Need Bar for:	Time Between Downward Pulses
Money	200
Entertainment	200
Human Contact	200
Food	200
Hygiene	100
Sleep	200

(Lower number = Need Bar drops faster)

ENTERTAINMENT NEEDS: BABETTE

Activity	Entertainment Satisfaction
Exercise	-5
Thrill	0
Combat Arena	0
Bar	0
Luxury Bar	8
Meditation Room	3
Library/Trainer	0
Piano	10
Relaxation Pod	6
Disco	5
Restaurant	7
Sauna	2
Jacuzzi	2
Observatory	0
Viewing Platform	0
Golf	-10
Zoo Exhibit	-10
Virtual Shop	6
Slot Machine	0

Entertainment Needs

A positive number for an activity means the Entertainment bar moves up. A negative number means the bar moves down. Zero (0) means the bar doesn't move at all in either direction.

Exercise = Rowing/Running Machines, Stairclimber

Thrill = Virtuality Chair, Zero-Gravity Playroom

Miscellaneous Attributes

Attribute	Rating	Attribute	Rating
Intelligence (0-10)	5	Happiness Boost from Pets (0-5)	5
(Higher number = Learns faster at Library or Trainer)		Litter Drop Rate (0-6)	1
Chance of Insanity (0 or 1-10)	3	(Higher number = Dirtier)	
(Higher number = Greater chance of going insane)		Rubbish Tolerance (0-5)	5
Greenery Benefit (0-10)	0	(Higher number = More intolerant)	
(Higher number = More satisfaction derived from plants)		Response to Counseling (1-10)	8
Noise Tolerance (0-5)	5	(Higher number = Faster back to sanity)	
(Higher number = More intolerant)		Response to Detention Center (1-10)	4
Expected Salary (0-6)	4	(Higher number = Faster back to sanity)	
(Higher number = Values money more)			

Basic Relationships

The following table lists Babette's starting relationship with each of the other 19 operatives in *Space Colony*. A positive number means the relationship is in the Friend range, with the highest possible friendship being 100. A negative number is in the Enemy range, with the deepest feeling of hatred at -100.

A relationship cannot drop any further than 50 points from the starting value listed in the table. However, it can rise clear up to 100 if properly nurtured.

BABETTE'S STARTING RELATIONSHIPS

Relationship with:	Rating
Venus	-20
Stig	-51
Tami	-32
Slim	-13
Dean	14
Candy	65
Billy Bob	-56
Nikolai	17
Daisy	-58
Captain	49
Vasilios	20
Hoshi	-21
Kita	-22
Mr. Zhang	13
Greg	-24
Nailer	30
Ashia	-66
Bhoomi	46
Barbara	14

Barbara Leechworth

Fast Facts

Age: 47	
Home: United States (Boston)	
Likes: Restaurant, Luxury Bar, Combat Arena	
Dislikes: Zoo Exhibit	
Special Needs: Financial	
Special Skills (Star Rating): None	
Basic Skills: Pharmaceuticals, Scavenging, Laser, Power, Oxygen, MediPrep	
Walking Speed: Fast	

Profile

Barbara Leechworth is corporate America personified. With her briefcase and padded shoulders, the woman could tear a hole through the Dallas Cowboys defensive line, then buy the team. For such an impressive woman, her technical skills are remarkably average—a born manager, obviously. But her six basic skills are helpful ones, and if you can keep her clean and compensated, Barbara will work hard for you.

Basic/Special Needs

Money is Barbara's special need. Her Financial Need bar drops at a steady, normal rate, but as it lowers, it sucks Barbara's overall Happiness right down, too. Consider raising colony wages a notch when Barbara comes on the scene.

2-9. Barbara has a special need for money.

Barbara doesn't need a lot of sleep, and her other needs are normal—except for Hygiene. Her desire for personal cleanliness verges on obsessive. She needs Human Contact more than the average, too, but an occasional Small Talk chat will keep her satisfied. Whatever task you assign Barbara, be sure a Personal Hygiene Pod is nearby!

Entertainment

Fine dining in the colony Restaurant is, by far, Barbara's favorite entertainment activity. She finds a number of other activities pleasurable, too—Piano, Luxury Bar, and Relaxation Pod foremost amongst them.

Like most of the other colonists who consider themselves well above blue-collar status, she finds Zoo Exhibits to be repulsive. To a lesser extent Barbara hates Disco, an activity that strikes her as onerous and rather plebian. She's wrapped so tight she won't even move when she's on the dance floor.

2-10. Barbara loves to dine in the colony Restaurant, so it fulfills two needs at once—Food and Entertainment.

Other Notable Attributes

She may be tight as a drum, but Barbara is the smartest gal on the base—as smart as Nikolai and second only to Mr. Zhang in the Intelligence category. So she's a very quick study when learning new skills in the Library. Unfortunately, her salary expectations are the highest on the base, too.

Relationships

Barbara's corporate brittleness doesn't sit well with certain colonists, especially Daisy, who sees her as the embodiment of porcine capitalism at its worst. Barbara doesn't start off well with Venus or Ashia either, and several other people will consider her an enemy right off the shuttle.

For some odd reason, Barbara's best initial relationships are with Greg and Nailer, the two crudest fellows on the base. Apparently, she has a thing for callow younger men.

Taking Barbara's Pulse

Here's a look at how quickly Barbara's six specific Need bars drop. The numbers represent how many units of game-time before the next "pulse" occurs for that Need bar. Each "pulse" lowers Barbara's Need bar a fraction. Thus, the lower the number, the faster the bar goes down. A zero (0) means the character has no need in this category.

Need Bar for:	Time Between Downward Pulses
Money	200
Entertainment	200
Human Contact	100
Food	200
Hygiene	50
Sleep	400

(Lower number = Need Bar drops faster)

Entertainment Needs

A positive number for an activity means the Entertainment bar moves up. A negative number means the bar moves down. Zero (0) means the bar doesn't move at all in either direction.

Special Needs

Financial

ENTERTAINMENT NEEDS: BARBARA

Activity	Entertainment Satisfaction Provided
Exercise	2
Thrill	0
Combat Arena	0
Bar	0
Luxury Bar	6
Meditation Room	0
Library/Trainer	0
Piano	6
Relaxation Pod	6
Disco	-4
Restaurant	10
Sauna	3
Jacuzzi	3
Observatory	0
Viewing Platform	0
Golf	4
Zoo Exhibit	-10
Virtual Shop	4
Slot Machine	4

Exercise = Rowing/Running Machines, Stairclimber

Thrill = Virtuality Chair, Zero-Gravity Playroom

Miscellaneous Attributes

Attribute	Rating
Intelligence (0-10)	9
(Higher number = Learns faster at Library or Trainer)	
Chance of Insanity (0 or 1-10)	2
(Higher number = Greater chance of going insane)	
Greenery Benefit (0-10)	0
(Higher number = More satisfaction derived from plants)	
Noise Tolerance (0-5)	2
(Higher number = More intolerant)	
Expected Salary (0-6)	6
(Higher number = Values money more)	
Happiness Boost from Pets (0-5)	2
Litter Drop Rate (0-6)	0
(Higher number = Dirtier)	
Rubbish Tolerance (0-5)	2
(Higher number = More intolerant)	
Response to Counseling (1-10)	5
(Higher number = Faster back to sanity)	
Response to Detention Center (1-10)	5
(Higher number = Faster back to sanity)	

Basic Relationships

The following table lists Barbara's starting relationship with each of the other 19 operatives in *Space Colony*. A positive number means the relationship is in the Friend range, with the highest possible friendship being 100. A negative number is in the Enemy range, with the deepest interpersonal loathing at -100. A relationship cannot drop any further than 50 points from the starting value listed in the table. However, it can rise clear up to 100 if properly nurtured.

BARBARA'S STARTING RELATIONSHIPS

Relationship with:	Rating
Venus	-59
Stig	-40
Tami	-11
Slim	2
Dean	-23
Candy	4
Billy Bob	15
Nikolai	6
Daisy	-87
Captain	-28
Vasilios	9
Hoshi	20
Kita	21
Mr. Zhang	22
Greg	43
Babette	14
Nailer	55
Ashia	-57
Bhoomi	38

Fast Facts

Age: 61	
Home: India	
Likes: Relaxation Pod, Golf	
Dislikes: Combat Arena	
Special Needs: Sleep	
Special Skills (Star Rating): None	
Basic Skills: Power, Oxygen, MediPrep, Cleaning, Maintenance	
Walking Speed: Slow	

Profile

Bhoomi is the upbeat, benevolent mother figure of the colony. Everybody loves her—even Babette and Barbara. She has only five basic-level skills, but Bhoomi's kind, warm presence is good for Human Contact, base-wide.

2-11. Bhoomi's special need, Sleep, is also her fastest dropping need. Keep her well rested.

Basic/Special Needs

Bhoomi's needs are normal across the board, except for Sleep, which she needs a lot of. As the Psychiatrist's Report says, "Her energy levels are low"—which is putting it mildly. This constant need to snooze can get in the way of steady work sometimes, but Bhoomi deserves a little slack, don't you think?

Entertainment

Bhoomi's favorite activity is a quiet session in the Relaxation Pod. Interestingly enough, her second favorite activity is... Golf. She also likes to shop and sit in the Jacuzzi or Sauna. Nothing provides her with a negative experience, but a number of activities leave her feeling unchanged.

Other Notable Attributes

Bhoomi loves plants and pets, and she places little value on money. Her quiet-loving demeanor leaves her with a low tolerance for noise when she's trying to sleep (which is often). Not surprisingly, she has zero chance of going insane.

2-12. Bhoomi's favorite facility is the Relaxation Pod.

Relationships

Bhoomi has warm feelings for everyone in the base when they first meet, and those feelings are reciprocated. She's particularly fond of Daisy and Mr. Zhang, who both share many of her attitudes toward life. She also likes Candy, of all people—probably the motherly impulse. Only three people are even capable of becoming Bhoomi's enemies over time—Barbara, Babette, and Stig.

Taking Bhoomi's Pulse

Here's a look at how quickly Bhoomi's six specific Need bars drop. The numbers represent how many units of game-time before the next "pulse" occurs for that Need bar. Each "pulse" lowers Bhoomi's Need bar a fraction. Thus, the lower the number, the faster the bar goes down. A zero (0) means the character has no need in this category.

Need Bar for:	Time Between Downward Pulses
Money	200
Entertainment	200
Human Contact	200
Food	200
Hygiene	200
Sleep	50

(Lower number = Need Bar drops faster)

Entertainment Needs

A positive number for an activity means the Entertainment bar moves up. A negative number means the bar moves down. Zero (0) means the bar doesn't move at all in either direction.

ENTERTAINMENT NEEDS: BHOOMI

Activity	Entertainment Satisfaction Provided
Exercise	0
Thrill	0
Combat Arena	0
Bar	0
Luxury Bar	0
Meditation Room	0
Library/Trainer	2
Piano	0
Relaxation Pod	9
Disco	2
Restaurant	2
Sauna	3
Jacuzzi	3
Observatory	0
Viewing Platform	0
Golf	6
Zoo Exhibit	0
Virtual Shop	4
Slot Machine	0

Exercise = Rowing/Running Machines, Stairclimber

Thrill = Virtuality Chair, Zero-Gravity Playroom

Special Needs

Sleep

Miscellaneous Attributes

Attribute	Rating
Intelligence (0-10)	4
(Higher number = Learns faster at Library or Trainer)	
Chance of Insanity (0 or 1-10)	0
(Higher number = Greater chance of going insane)	
Greenery Benefit (0-10)	6
(Higher number = More satisfaction derived from plants)	
Noise Tolerance (0-5)	4
(Higher number = More intolerant)	
Expected Salary (0-6)	2
(Higher number = Values money more)	
Happiness Boost from Pets (0-5)	4
Litter Drop Rate (0-6)	0
(Higher number = Dirtier)	
Rubbish Tolerance (0-5)	3
(Higher number = More intolerant)	
Response to Counseling (1-10)	8
(Higher number = Faster back to sanity)	
Response to Detention Center (1-10)	6
(Higher number = Faster back to sanity)	

Basic Relationships

The following table lists Bhoomi's starting relationship with each of the other 19 operatives in *Space Colony*. A positive number means the relationship is in the Friend range, with the highest possible friendship being 100. A negative number is in the Enemy range, with the deepest interpersonal loathing at -100. A relationship cannot drop any further than 50 points from the starting value listed in the table. However, it can rise clear up to 100 if properly nurtured.

BHOOMI'S STARTING RELATIONSHIPS

Relationship with:	Rating		Relationship with:	Rating
Venus	61		Vasilios	61
Stig	42		Hoshi	62
Tami	63		Kita	63
Slim	64		Mr. Zhang	74
Dean	67		Greg	65
Candy	76		Babette	46
Billy Bob	60		Nailer	57
Nikolai	61		Ashia	68
Daisy	79		Barbara	38
Captain	60			

Billy Bob Perkins

Fast Facts

Age:	33
Home:	United States (Tennessee)
Likes:	Zoo Exhibits
Dislikes:	Combat Arena
Special Needs:	Food
Special Skills (Star Rating):	Chicken Extraction (4)
Basic Skills:	Nutrient Extraction, Weeding, Cleaning, Maintenance
Walking Speed:	Average

Profile

Sure, he's a little dim. But Billy Bob is a heck of a nice guy—and he's the only Space Colony operative who comes to your base with a 4-star Skill level right out of the shuttle. This man can farm and process Space Chickens with stunning efficiency. He also brings some needed basic-level Skills to the colony.

Basic/Special Needs

Being around chicken products all day long, Billy Bob has a high tolerance for unhygienic conditions. Thus, his Hygiene Need is half the standard. And all the long hours on the farm back home in Tennessee have trained him to need less sleep. But because Billy Bob's a big, hardworking fellow, Food is a special need—when hungry, he's particularly unhappy about it. Feed the boy! Note also that his Food Need bar drops four times faster than the average, making his special need also his fastest-dropping need. So you'd better keep an eye on it.

2-13. Billy Bob was born to be a chicken farmer.

Entertainment

Dang, Billy Bob *loves* the zoo. He's a farm boy, so he can derive the deepest satisfaction (a full 10!) from staring at all them animals. However, despite his mild-mannered, low-key personality (or perhaps *because* of it), Billy Bob can also enjoy thrill-oriented fun, such as the Zero-Gravity Playroom and Virtuality Chair. He's also particularly fond of golfing, working off his heft on the exercise equipment, or just taking a breather in the Sauna or Jacuzzi. If none of that is available, Billy Bob can amuse himself by looking at stuff in the Virtual Shop.

2-14. Billy Bob's favorite activity is staring at Zoo Exhibits.

Other Notable Attributes

Billy Bob is not a good learner, to put it charitably. He has a fondness for greenery around the base, and he sleeps like a rock, with high tolerance for noise.

Relationships

Who couldn't get along with such a nice, unassuming fellow? Well, as it turns out, a number of people—Babette, Slim, Greg, and Mr. Zhang all start out at odds with Billy Bob for various reasons. But most others hold him in good regard on first meeting, especially Nailer, Venus, Ashia, and Bhoomi.

Taking Billy Bob's Pulse

Here's a look at how quickly Billy Bob's six specific Need bars drop. The numbers represent how many units of game-time before the next "pulse" occurs for that Need bar. Each "pulse" lowers Billy Bob's Need bar a fraction. Thus, the lower the number, the faster the bar goes down. A zero (0) means the character has no need in this category.

Need Bar for:	Time Between Downward Pulses
Money	200
Entertainment	100
Human Contact	100
Food	50
Hygiene	400
Sleep	400

(Lower number = Need Bar drops faster)

ENTERTAINMENT NEEDS: BILLY BOB

Activity	Entertainment Satisfaction Provided
Exercise	4
Thrill	6
Combat Arena	0
Bar	0
Luxury Bar	0
Meditation Room	0
Library/Trainer	0
Piano	2
Relaxation Pod	0
Disco	0
Restaurant	0
Sauna	4
Jacuzzi	4
Observatory	0
Viewing Platform	0
Golf	5
Zoo Exhibit	10
Virtual Shop	4
Slot Machine	0

Entertainment Needs

A positive number for an activity means the Entertainment bar moves up. A negative number means the bar moves down. Zero (0) means the bar doesn't move at all in either direction.

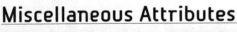

Exercise = Rowing/Running Machines, Stairclimber
Thrill = Virtuality Chair, Zero-Gravity Playroom

Miscellaneous Attributes

Attribute	Rating
Intelligence (0-10)	1
(Higher number = Learns faster at Library or Trainer)	
Chance of Insanity (0 or 1-10)	0
(Higher number = Greater chance of going insane)	
Greenery Benefit (0-10)	4
(Higher number = More satisfaction derived from plants)	
Noise Tolerance (0-5)	1
(Higher number = More intolerant)	
Expected Salary (0-6)	2
(Higher number = Values money more)	

Happiness Boost from Pets (0-5)	1
Litter Drop Rate (0-6)	0
(Higher number = Dirtier)	
Rubbish Tolerance (0-5)	1
(Higher number = More intolerant)	
Response to Counseling (1-10)	2
(Higher number = Faster back to sanity)	
Response to Detention Center (1-10)	8
(Higher number = Faster back to sanity)	

Basic Relationships

The following table lists Billy Bob's starting relationship with each of the other 19 operatives in *Space Colony*. A positive number means the relationship is in the Friend range, with the highest possible friendship being 100. A negative number is in the Enemy range, with the deepest interpersonal loathing at -100. A relationship cannot drop any further than 50 points from the starting value listed in the table. However, it can rise clear up to 100 if properly nurtured.

BILLY BOB'S STARTING RELATIONSHIPS

Relationship with:	Rating
Venus	75
Stig	41
Tami	12
Slim	-43
Dean	24
Candy	45
Nikolai	42
Daisy	49
Captain	37
Vasilios	46
Hoshi	7
Kita	8
Mr. Zhang	-19
Greg	-22
Babette	-56
Nailer	81
Ashia	67
Bhoomi	60
Barbara	15

Candy Simpson

Fast Facts

Age: 24
Home: United States (California)
Likes: Shopping, Restaurant, Disco
Special Needs: Human Contact
Special Skills (Star Rating): None
Basic Skills: Cleaning
Walking Speed: Average

Profile

Candy is just, like, totally way cute! But the only two things she brings to your colony are a basic Cleaning skill and a burning need to, like, just chill and chat, dude! Unlike Tami, who has other skills, Candy is destined to do nothing but work the Cleaning Post until you train her at something else!

But that's okay! Good base cleanliness raises everyone's spirits! Remember, when colonists walk through litter piles, their Hygiene bar drops!

Basic/Special Needs

Tired of exclamation points? Candy's actually a fairly well adjusted young woman for a shopping cheerleader from California. Her needs for sleep, cleanliness, and money all are normal. But she does require a lot of Human Contact and Entertainment. On top of that, Human Contact is a special need, meaning as it goes down, Candy's overall Happiness bar drops precipitously. So keep her "small-talking" and give her plenty of Friendship chats in the Social Area, too.

2-15. Keep Candy communicating with other colonists. The more friends she has, the better.

Get Tami and Candy on friendly terms. (They start out at –18.) These two can help meet each other's overwhelming Human Contact needs by engaging in regular Small Talk or Friendship encounters. This frees up other colonists to go about their business.

2-16. Candy's favorite activity is browsing in the Virtual Shop.

Entertainment

Candy makes up for her lack of Skills by being easily entertained, making her easy to manage. Her favorite activity, by far, is browsing the Virtual Shop. But she also gets high satisfaction from lounging at the Luxury Bar, dancing at the Disco, or dining on the fine extracted-chicken products at the Restaurant.

She has only slightly less fun in the Virtuality Chair or the Jacuzzi. In fact, Candy finds pleasure in almost every single Entertainment facility in the colony. Only the Combat Arena, Meditation Room, Observatory, Viewing Platform, and Library/Trainer leave her feeling sort of neutral. Everything else is, like, so much fun, like, totally!

Other Notable Attributes

Candy's prone to going mad if her Happiness bar hits the red. If that happens, she gets faster results from the Counseling Robot than she does from the Detention Center.

Relationships

Babette and Bhoomi are Candy's surefire friends, come hell or high water or, like, whatever! She starts off well with Slim, Venus, Ashia, and Billy Bob, too. Tami and Nailer begin as Candy's enemies, though, and brittle Barbara can barely tolerate her.

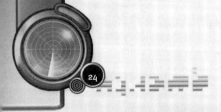

Taking Candy's Pulse

Here's a look at how quickly Candy's six specific Need bars drop. The numbers represent how many units of game-time before the next "pulse" occurs for that Need bar. Each "pulse" lowers Candy's Need bar a fraction Thus, the lower the number, the faster the bar goes down. A zero (o) means the character has no need in this category.

Need Bar for:	Time Between Downward Pulses
Money	200
Entertainment	50
Human Contact	50
Food	400
Hygiene	200
Sleep	200

(Lower number = Need Bar drops faster)

Entertainment Needs

A positive number for an activity means the Entertainment bar moves up. A negative number means the bar moves down. Zero (o) means the bar doesn't move at all in either direction.

ENTERTAINMENT NEEDS: CANDY

Activity	Entertainment Satisfaction Provided
Exercise	4
Thrill	6
Combat Arena	0
Bar	4
Luxury Bar	8
Meditation Room	0
Library/Trainer	0
Piano	2
Relaxation Pod	5
Disco	7
Restaurant	7
Sauna	4
Jacuzzi	6
Observatory	0
Viewing Platform	0
Golf	4
Zoo Exhibit	5
Virtual Shop	10
Slot Machine	3

Miscellaneous Attributes

Attribute	Rating	Attribute	Rating
Intelligence (0-10)	2	Happiness Boost from Pets (0-5)	3
(Higher number = Learns faster at Library or Trainer)		Litter Drop Rate (0-6)	1
Chance of Insanity (0 or 1-10)	8	(Higher number = Dirtier)	
(Higher number = Greater chance of going insane)		Rubbish Tolerance (0-5)	2
Greenery Benefit (0-10)	4	(Higher number = More intolerant)	
(Higher number = More satisfaction derived from plants)		Response to Counseling (1-10)	6
Noise Tolerance (0-5)	3	(Higher number = Faster back to sanity)	
(Higher number = More intolerant)		Response to Detention Center (1-10)	4
Expected Salary (0-6)	2	(Higher number = Faster back to sanity)	
(Higher number = Values money more)			

Basic Relationships

The following table lists Candy's starting relationship with each of the other 19 operatives in *Space Colony*. A positive number means the relationship is in the Friend range, with the highest possible friendship being 100. A negative number is in the Enemy range, with the deepest interpersonal loathing at -100. A relationship cannot drop any further than 50 points from the starting value listed in the table. However, it can rise clear up to 100 if properly nurtured.

CANDY'S STARTING RELATIONSHIPS

Relationship with:	Rating	Relationship with:	Rating
Venus	46	Hoshi	6
Stig	17	Kita	7
Tami	-18	Mr. Zhang	18
Slim	49	Greg	11
Dean	20	Babette	65
Billy Bob	45	Nailer	-10
Nikolai	21	Ashia	46
Daisy	38	Bhoomi	76
Captain	26	Barbara	4
Vasilios	25		

Capt. Charles Wilmington

Fast Facts

Age: 55	
Home: England	
Likes: Gambling, Golf, Sauna	
Dislikes: Shopping	
Special Needs: None	
Special Skills (Star Rating): Laser (3)	
Basic Skills: Mining, Nutrient Extraction, Space Gas, Weeding, Power, Oxygen, Cleaning, Maintenance	
Walking Speed: Very Fast!	

Profile

This old chap is old-school all the way—which certainly has its good points. Charles has an ex-military man's deadeye skill with the Manned Laser, and he brings numerous other basic Skills to the colony. He has no special needs, so his overall Happiness tends to be steady, without sudden, precipitous drops. And he's the fastest walker in the colony.

Basic/Special Needs

Charles is a little picky about his hygiene and requires a few more doses of quality entertainment than the average fellow. But other than those minor quirks, he's solid as a cricket bat. The old military training gives him an impeccable work ethic, enhanced by the fact that he requires only about half the normal amount of sleep.

2-17. Capt. Charles is handy with the Manned Laser turret.

Entertainment

Good Captain Wilmington is easy to keep amused, too. He's got a slight obsession with Slot Machines, and he's quite fond of Golf, the Sauna and Jacuzzi, and workouts on the Exercise Machines (in that order). Charles doesn't mind a little cocktail now and again, and gets solid pleasure from dining in the colony Restaurant. He even enjoys a turn on the Disco floor, looking pretty spry for a relic of more chivalrous days.

However, the man bitterly resents shopping. Nothing could be more mortifying, really.

2-18. Charles' favorite activity is the Slot Machine.

Other Notable Attributes

The Captain's intelligence is on the high end, so he can be a fairly quick study if you need him to pitch in with a new skill. He's rather fond of pets; he has a 50 percent chance of going nuts when his Happiness drops into the red; and his salary demands are a bit on the high side, although not unreasonable.

Relationships

Charles enjoys jolly good relationships with Greg and Stig, two guys who can relate to the Captain's sense of male esprit de corps. He also admires Bhoomi and has a fine gentleman's regard for Babette. Slim and Nailer get on his nerves right away, though, and he has initial dislike for Barbara and Daisy—two women who just don't respect old-school thinking.

Taking the Captain's Pulse

Here's a look at how quickly Charles's six specific Need bars drop. The numbers represent how many units of game-time before the next "pulse" occurs for that Need bar. Each "pulse" lowers Charles's Need bar a fraction. Thus, the lower the number, the faster the bar goes down. A zero (0) means the character has no need in this category.

Need Bar for:	Time Between Downward Pulses
Money	200
Entertainment	100
Human Contact	200
Food	200
Hygiene	100
Sleep	400

(Lower number = Need Bar drops faster)

ENTERTAINMENT NEEDS: CHARLES

Activity	Entertainment
Satisfaction ProvidedExercise	6
Thrill	0
Combat Arena	0
Bar	5
Luxury Bar	5
Meditation Room	0
Library/Trainer	0
Piano	0
Relaxation Pod	0
Disco	2
Restaurant	5
Sauna	8
Jacuzzi	7
Observatory	0
Viewing Platform	0
Golf	8
Zoo Exhibit	0
Virtual Shop	-10
Slot Machine	10

Entertainment Needs

A positive number for an activity means the Entertainment bar moves up. A negative number means the bar moves down. Zero (0) means the bar doesn't move at all in either direction.

Exercise = Rowing/Running Machines, Stairclimber
Thrill = Virtuality Chair, Zero-Gravity Playroom

Miscellaneous Attributes

Attribute	Rating
Intelligence (0-10)	6
(Higher number = Learns faster at Library or Trainer)	
Chance of Insanity (0 or 1-10)	5
(Higher number = Greater chance of going insane)	
Greenery Benefit (0-10)	1
(Higher number = More satisfaction derived from plants)	
Noise Tolerance (0-5)	4
(Higher number = More intolerant)	
Expected Salary (0-6)	4
(Higher number = Values money more)	

Attribute	Rating
Happiness Boost from Pets (0-5)	4
Litter Drop Rate (0-6)	2
(Higher number = Dirtier)	
Rubbish Tolerance (0-5)	4
(Higher number = More intolerant)	
Response to Counseling (1-10)	7
(Higher number = Faster back to sanity)	
Response to Detention Center (1-10)	7
(Higher number = Faster back to sanity)	

Basic Relationships

The following table lists the Captain's starting relationship with each of the other 19 operatives in *Space Colony*. A positive number means the relationship is in the Friend range, with the highest possible friendship being 100. A negative number is in the Enemy range, with the deepest interpersonal loathing at -100. A relationship cannot drop any further than 50 points from the starting value listed in the table. However, it can rise clear up to 100 if properly nurtured.

CHARLES'S STARTING RELATIONSHIPS

Relationship with:	Rating
Venus	31
Stig	62
Tami	33
Slim	-34
Dean	25
Candy	26
Billy Bob	37
Nikolai	38
Daisy	-19
Vasilios	19
Hoshi	-20
Kita	-21
Mr. Zhang	12
Greg	65
Babette	49
Nailer	-14
Ashia	4
Bhoomi4	60
Barbara	-28

Daisy Willowreed

Fast Facts

Age: 31	
Home: United States (Montana)	
Likes: Meditation Room, Observatory	
Dislikes: Combat Arena, Zoo Exhibit, Golf	
Special Needs: None	
Special Skills (Star Rating): Bio Research (2)	
Basic Skills: Nutrient Extraction, Pharmaceuticals, Power, Oxygen, Cleaning, Maintenance	
Walking Speed: Average	

Profile

The Psychiatrist's Report labels her a "liability," but Daisy brings a decent array of Skills to the table, including a 2-star rating in Bio Research. And her basic Skills prove helpful in keeping your colony running smoothly.

Basic/Special Needs

Thin as her last name, Daisy requires an inordinate amount of sleep—four times the usual. On the other hand, her deep respect for "natural states of being" means she doesn't mind skipping a shower here and there. And Daisy's low metabolism keeps both her Food intake and Entertainment needs fairly low, too. This makes up for all the naps she has to take.

Entertainment

Daisy particularly enjoys contemplative pursuits, such as *ooommm-ing* in the Meditation Room or stargazing in the Observatory. To a lesser extent she digs an occasional Disco dance or just vegging out in the Relaxation Pod. Stints in the Sauna or Jacuzzi can raise her communal spirits, as can a sit at the Bar (but not the Luxury Bar, which reeks of rapacious capitalism and investment income).

Warning, though: Daisy absolutely loathes violence and cheap thrills, whether real or simulated. So she's disgusted by the Combat Arena, as well as by the sense-battering experience of the Virtuality Chair or Zero-Gravity Playroom. She also hates perversions of nature, such as Golf or Zoo Exhibits. And shopping is about as appealing to her as an herbicide facial.

2-19. Daisy loves the Meditation Room.

2-20. Plants really brighten up Daisy's day.

Other Notable Attributes

Daisy gets the highest possible satisfaction from exposure to greenery. If she's in your colony, drop in a few houseplants to boost her overall sense of cosmic wellbeing.

Relationships

Daisy rivals Barbara for the number of colonists she starts off badly with—nine in the negative numbers. She hates money-grubbers like Barbara, of course, and has pretty sour feelings for Stig, Slim, Babette, and Greg, too. Daisy only can't-miss friendships are with Bhoomi and the oddly vacant Vasilios.

Taking Daisy's Pulse

Here's a look at how quickly Daisy's six specific Need bars drop. The numbers represent how many units of game-time before the next "pulse" occurs for that Need bar. Each "pulse" lowers Daisy's Need bar a tick. Thus, the lower the number, the faster the bar goes down. A zero (0) means the character has no need in this category.

Need Bar for:	Time Between Downward Pulses
Money	200
Entertainment	400
Human Contact	100
Food	400
Hygiene	600
Sleep	50

(Lower number = Need Bar drops faster)

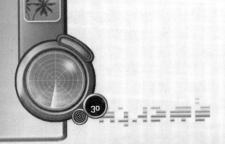

Entertainment Needs

A positive number for an activity means the Entertainment bar moves up. A negative number means the bar moves down. Zero (0) means the bar doesn't move at all in either direction.

ENTERTAINMENT NEEDS: DAISY

Activity	Entertainment Satisfaction Provided
Exercise	2
Thrill	-4
Combat Arena	-4
Bar	2
Luxury Bar	0
Meditation Room	8
Library/Trainer	0
Piano	0
Relaxation Pod	5
Disco	4
Restaurant	0
Sauna	3
Jacuzzi	3
Observatory	8
Viewing Platform	0
Golf	-4
Zoo Exhibit	-4
Virtual Shop	-4
Slot Machine	0

Exercise = Rowing/Running Machines, Stairclimber
Thrill = Virtuality Chair, Zero-Gravity Playroom

Miscellaneous Attributes

Attribute	Rating
Intelligence (0-10)	4
(Higher number = Learns faster at Library or Trainer)	
Chance of Insanity (0 or 1-10)	2
(Higher number = Greater chance of going insane)	
Greenery Benefit (0-10)	10
(Higher number = More satisfaction derived from plants)	
Noise Tolerance (0-5)	1
(Higher number = More intolerant)	
Expected Salary (0-6)	1
(Higher number = Values money more)	
Happiness Boost from Pets (0-5)	1
Litter Drop Rate (0-6)	0
(Higher number = Dirtier)	
Rubbish Tolerance (0-5)	1
(Higher number = More intolerant)	
Response to Counseling (1-10)	10
(Higher number = Faster back to sanity)	
Response to Detention Center (1-10)	2
(Higher number = Faster back to sanity)	

Basic Relationships

The following table lists Daisy's starting relationship with each of the other 19 operatives in *Space Colony*. A positive number means the relationship is in the Friend range, with the highest possible friendship being 100. A negative number is in the Enemy range, with the deepest interpersonal loathing at -100. A relationship cannot drop any further than 50 points from the starting value listed in the table. However, it can rise clear up to 100 if properly nurtured.

DAISY'S STARTING RELATIONSHIPS

Relationship with:	Rating	Relationship with:	Rating
Venus	43	Hoshi	39
Stig	-64	Kita	40
Tami	-35	Mr. Zhang	-21
Slim	-46	Greg	-44
Dean	47	Babette	-58
Candy	38	Nailer	20
Billy Bob	49	Ashia	49
Nikolai	-10	Bhoomi	79
Captain	-19	Barbara	-87
Vasilios	68		

Fast Facts

Age: 25	
Home: United States (Los Angeles)	
Likes: Sport, Golf, Learning	
Dislikes: Bar	
Special Needs: Hygiene	
Special Skills (Star Rating): MediPrep (3)	
Basic Skills: Pharmaceuticals, Weeding, Power, Oxygen	
Walking Speed: Fast	

Profile

Dean is cool, despite having gone to Harvard. A highly skilled MediPrep technician (3 stars!), he's a critically important member of your team in the later Catherwood missions. (Without quickly prepped Medi Bays, your colonists become mere virus food.) He's also got a basic skill level in Pharmaceuticals, always useful.

Basic/Special Needs

Dean's only drawback is his cleanliness phobia—the guy needs to shower *way* too often, four times the normal. And Hygiene is a special need, too, meaning his overall Happiness is more affected by a dropping Hygiene bar. So keep the man clean, will you?

2-21. Dean has personal hygiene issues. Send him to the showers regularly.

Entertainment

For Entertainment, Dean gets the biggest charge out of athletic training and golf. Whenever his Entertainment bar drops low, send him to the nearest exercise machine for a serious workout, or to hit the links for a quick round. He also enjoys the post-workout relaxation of a Sauna, Jacuzzi, or Meditation Room, and a good meal in the base Restaurant. (See the next section for a unique source of entertainment for Dean.)

2-22. Dean's a workout warrior, and he loves it. Exercise is his favorite form of entertainment.

Other Notable Attributes

Dean is a highly motivated learner. His academic pedigree is no fluke—the man loves to study in the Library. Indeed, pulling all-nighters is his specialty; Dean needs little sleep. Whether you upgrade his current skills or teach him something new, Dean does it fast. Even better, he enjoys it! A good study session actually boosts Dean's Entertainment score.

Walking through a litter-strewn base also lays a big hit on Dean's overall Happiness. His low rubbish tolerance goes hand-in-hand with his Hygiene obsession.

Relationships

Dean starts off with solid friends in Bhoomi, Ashia, and Venus. But his initial relationship is particularly rocky with Tami, Kita, Hoshi, and Barbara.

Taking Dean's Pulse

Here's a look at how quickly Dean's six specific Need bars drop. The numbers represent how many units of game-time before the next "pulse" occurs for that Need bar. Each "pulse" lowers Dean's Need bar a fraction. Thus, the lower the number, the faster the bar goes down. A zero (0) means the character has no need in this category.

Need Bar for:	Time Between Downward Pulses
Money	200
Entertainment	200
Human Contact	200
Food	200
Hygiene	50
Sleep	400

(Lower number = Need Bar drops faster)

Entertainment Needs

A positive number for an activity means the Entertainment bar moves up. A negative number means the bar moves down. Zero (0) means the bar doesn't move at all in either direction.

ENTERTAINMENT NEEDS: DEAN

Activity	Entertainment Satisfaction Provided
Exercise	9
Thrill	2
Combat Arena	2
Bar	0
Luxury Bar	0
Meditation Room	4
Library/Trainer	5
Piano	0
Relaxation Pod	0
Disco	1
Restaurant	4
Sauna	4
Jacuzzi	4
Observatory	0
Viewing Platform	0
Golf	8
Zoo Exhibit	0
Virtual Shop	1
Slot Machine	0

Exercise = Rowing/Running Machines, Stairclimber
Thrill = Virtuality Chair, Zero-Gravity Playroom

Miscellaneous Attributes

Attribute	Rating
Intelligence (0-10)	8
(Higher number = Learns faster at Library or Trainer)	
Chance of Insanity (0 or 1-10)	2
(Higher number = Greater chance of going insane)	
Greenery Benefit (0-10)	2
(Higher number = More satisfaction derived from plants)	
Noise Tolerance (0-5)	2
(Higher number = More intolerant)	
Expected Salary (0-6)	2
(Higher number = Values money more)	
Happiness Boost from Pets (0-5)	2
Litter Drop Rate (0-6)	0
(Higher number = Dirtier)	
Rubbish Tolerance (0-5)	4
(Higher number = More intolerant)	
Response to Counseling (1-10)	8
(Higher number = Faster back to sanity)	
Response to Detention Center (1-10)	4
(Higher number = Faster back to sanity)	

Basic Relationships

The following table lists Dean's starting relationship with each of the other 19 operatives in *Space Colony*. A positive number means the relationship is in the Friend range, with the highest possible friendship being 100. A negative number is in the Enemy range, with the deepest interpersonal loathing at -100. A relationship cannot drop any further than 50 points from the starting value listed in the table. However, it can rise clear up to 100 if properly nurtured.

DEAN'S STARTING RELATIONSHIPS

Relationship with:	Rating	Relationship with:	Rating
Venus	54	Hoshi	-25
Stig	32	Kita	-26
Tami	-43	Mr. Zhang	27
Slim	-21	Greg	-10
Candy	20	Babette	14
Billy Bob	24	Nailer	-19
Nikolai	10	Ashia	65
Daisy	47	Bhoomi	67
Captain	25	Barbara	-23
Vasilios	14		

Fast Facts

Age: 29	
Home: United States (New Jersey)	
Likes: Jacuzzi, Luxury Bar, Golf	
Dislikes: Zoo Exhibits, Shopping	
Special Needs: Human Contact	
Special Skills (Star Rating): Mining (1)	
Basic Skills: Repair, Space Gas, Laser, Power, Oxygen	
Walking Speed: Average	

Profile

Venus' description is nice and succinct: "What can I say? Greg's a jerk." This is certainly true from a female perspective. Greg's pretty sure women want him. He's just sorry he can't provide service to all. He brings a one-star Mining Skill to the base, plus several good basic skills, such as Laser, Repair, and Space Gas. He also brings his ego, which is roughly the size of the third gas giant in the Mgeni System.

Basic/Special Needs

Greg has overwhelming needs for both Entertainment and Human Contact. Keeping Greg on the prowl for both (especially Human Contact, which is also a special need for him) sometimes gets in the way of a steady work output, but at least you don't have to worry about his Hygiene. *Greg* certainly doesn't worry about it. He can go a very long time between showers.

2-23. Greg has an almost pathological need for human contact.

2-24. Greg finds a Jacuzzi the highest form of entertainment known to man.

Entertainment

Greg really hates shopping, deeply, and he thinks Zoos are for lowbrow chumps and losers. Luxury Bars are nice, and a good manly round of Golf is cool enough. But nothing at all can compare to the deep, muscle-penetrating satisfaction of a hot soak in the Jacuzzi. Greg would live in the living waters, if he could.

Other Notable Attributes

Middle of the road in most other attributes, Greg is tolerant of both noise and rubbish (no surprise here given his attendance to personal hygiene).

Relationships

Chauvinist Greg starts out on the bad side of well over half the 20 colonists in *Space Colony*, particularly Venus, Ashia, Daisy, Hoshi, Kita—see a pattern here? His only true friends are the motherly Bhoomi (someone he has no desire to hit on), the Captain, and Tami (who has a weak spot in her heart for scoundrels of all stripes).

Taking Greg's Pulse

Here's a look at how quickly Greg's six specific Need bars drop. The numbers represent how many units of game-time before the next "pulse" occurs for that Need bar. Each "pulse" lowers Greg's Need bar a fraction. Thus, the lower the number, the faster the bar goes down. A zero (0) means the character has no need in this category.

Need Bar for:	Time Between Downward Pulses
Money	200
Entertainment	25
Human Contact	25
Food	100
Hygiene	1000
Sleep	400

(Lower number = Need Bar drops faster)

ENTERTAINMENT NEEDS: GREG

Activity	Entertainment Satisfaction Provided
Exercise	2
Thrill	2
Combat Arena	0
Bar	4
Luxury Bar	7
Meditation Room	0
Library/Trainer	0
Piano	0
Relaxation Pod	7
Disco	3
Restaurant	5
Sauna	5
Jacuzzi	10
Observatory	0
Viewing Platform	0
Golf	7
Zoo Exhibit	-10
Virtual Shop	-10
Slot Machine	4

Entertainment Needs

A positive number for an activity means the Entertainment bar moves up. A negative number means the bar moves down. Zero (0) means the bar doesn't move at all in either direction.

Exercise = Rowing/Running Machines, Stairclimber

Thrill = Virtuality Chair, Zero-Gravity Playroom

Miscellaneous Attributes

Attribute	Rating
Intelligence (0-10)	5
(Higher number = Learns faster at Library or Trainer)	
Chance of Insanity (0 or 1-10)	6
(Higher number = Greater chance of going insane)	
Greenery Benefit (0-10)	1
(Higher number = More satisfaction derived from plants)	
Noise Tolerance (0-5)	1
(Higher number = More intolerant)	
Expected Salary (0-6)	3
(Higher number = Values money more)	

Attribute	Rating
Happiness Boost from Pets (0-5)	1
Litter Drop Rate (0-6)	3
(Higher number = Dirtier)	
Rubbish Tolerance (0-5)	1
(Higher number = More intolerant)	
Response to Counseling (1-10)	5
(Higher number = Faster back to sanity)	
Response to Detention Center (1-10)	5
(Higher number = Faster back to sanity)	

Basic Relationships

The following table lists Greg's starting relationship with each of the other 19 operatives in *Space Colony*. A positive number means the relationship is in the Friend range, with the highest possible friendship being 100. A negative number is in the Enemy range, with the deepest interpersonal loathing at -100. A relationship cannot drop any further than 50 points from the starting value listed in the table. However, it can rise clear up to 100 if properly nurtured.

GREG'S STARTING RELATIONSHIPS

Relationship with:	Rating	Relationship with:	Rating
Venus	-66	Vasilios	16
Stig	-37	Hoshi	-37
Tami	64	Kita	-38
Slim	-39	Mr. Zhang	-19
Dean	-10	Babette	-24
Candy	11	Nailer	-39
Billy Bob	-22	Ashia	-55
Nikolai	13	Bhoomi	65
Daisy	-44	Barbara	43
Captain	65		

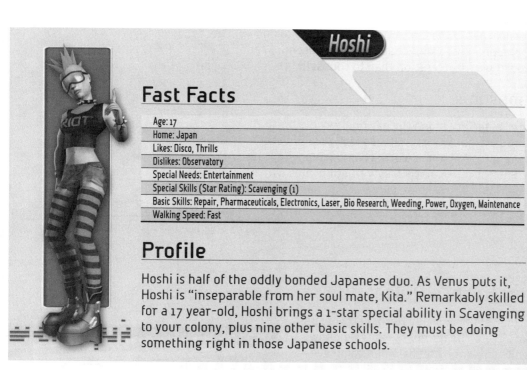

Hoshi

Fast Facts

Age: 17	
Home: Japan	
Likes: Disco, Thrills	
Dislikes: Observatory	
Special Needs: Entertainment	
Special Skills (Star Rating): Scavenging (1)	
Basic Skills: Repair, Pharmaceuticals, Electronics, Laser, Bio Research, Weeding, Power, Oxygen, Maintenance	
Walking Speed: Fast	

Profile

Hoshi is half of the oddly bonded Japanese duo. As Venus puts it, Hoshi is "inseparable from her soul mate, Kita." Remarkably skilled for a 17 year-old, Hoshi brings a 1-star special ability in Scavenging to your colony, plus nine other basic skills. They must be doing something right in those Japanese schools.

Basic/Special Needs

Hoshi is easily manageable, with slow-dropping needs for Entertainment, Food, and Hygiene. Don't let that lull you into ignoring the Entertainment need, because it falls in the special category. Hoshi's Human Contact need is in overdrive, but regular small talk with Kita can keep both girls in line.

Entertainment

Like Kita, Hoshi is addicted to Disco. Both girls derive the highest satisfaction from flapping across the dance floor. Hoshi also enjoys thrill-seeker fun in the Virtuality Chair or Zero Gravity Playroom, and can find satisfaction in a little Virtual Shop browsing, too.

Despite the fun she gets from working up a sweat on the Disco floor, Hoshi finds outcome-oriented exercise to be very boring and uncool.

2-25. Hoshi's favorite outlet is Disco dancing.

Other Notable Attributes

Hoshi has slightly above-average intelligence, so she can be a good learner in the Library. If she happens to go mad when unhappy (a slim chance), Hoshi responds far better to simple incarceration than to counseling.

Relationships

Kita scores a perfect 100 in Hoshi's relationship book. Most others are not so fortunate. In fact, only Bhoomi has anything resembling a warm relationship with Hoshi to start. She has particularly frosty relationships with Mr. Zhang, Tami, and Nikolai, plus starting negative relations with nine other colonists!

2-26. Hoshi and Kita are nearly psychological clones.

Taking Hoshi's Pulse

Here's a look at how quickly Hoshi's six specific Need bars drop. The numbers represent how many units of game-time between each "pulse" for that Need bar. A pulse lowers Hoshi's Need bar a fraction. Thus, the lower the number, the faster the bar goes down. A zero (0) means the character has no need in this category.

Need Bar for:	Time Between Downward Pulses
Money	200
Entertainment	400
Human Contact	50
Food	400
Hygiene	400
Sleep	200

(Lower number = Need Bar drops faster)

Entertainment Needs

A positive number for an activity means the Entertainment bar moves up. A negative number means the bar moves down. Zero (0) means the bar doesn't move at all in either direction.

ENTERTAINMENT NEEDS: HOSHI

Activity	Entertainment Satisfaction Provided	Activity	Entertainment Satisfaction Provided
Exercise	-2	Restaurant	0
Thrill	6	Sauna	2
Combat Arena	1	Jacuzzi	2
Bar	0	Observatory	0
Luxury Bar	0	Viewing Platform	0
Meditation Room	0	Golf	2
Library/Trainer	0	Zoo Exhibit	0
Piano	0	Virtual Shop	4
Relaxation Pod	0	Slot Machine	0
Disco	10		

Exercise = Rowing/Running Machines, Stairclimber

Thrill = Virtuality Chair, Zero-Gravity Playroom

Miscellaneous Attributes

Attribute	Rating
Intelligence (0-10)	6
(Higher number = Learns faster at Library or Trainer)	
Chance of Insanity (0 or 1-10)	2
(Higher number = Greater chance of going insane)	
Greenery Benefit (0-10)	2
(Higher number = More satisfaction derived from plants)	
Noise Tolerance (0-5)	0
(Higher number = More intolerant)	
Expected Salary (0-6)	3
(Higher number = Values money more)	
Happiness Boost from Pets (0-5)	0
Litter Drop Rate (0-6)	2
(Higher number = Dirtier)	
Rubbish Tolerance (0-5)	2
(Higher number = More intolerant)	
Response to Counseling (1-10)	1
(Higher number = Faster back to sanity)	
Response to Detention Center (1-10)	10
(Higher number = Faster back to sanity)	

Basic Relationships

The following table lists Hoshi's starting relationship with each of the other 19 operatives in *Space Colony*. A positive number means the relationship is in the Friend range, with the highest possible friendship being 100. A negative number is in the Enemy range, with the deepest interpersonal loathing at -100. A relationship cannot drop any further than 50 points from the starting value listed in the table. However, it can rise clear up to 100 if properly nurtured.

HOSHI'S STARTING RELATIONSHIPS

Relationship with:	Rating	Relationship with:	Rating
Venus	-1	Vasilios	-11
Stig	-32	Kita	100
Tami	-63	Mr. Zhang	-74
Slim	-14	Greg	-37
Dean	-25	Babette	-21
Candy	6	Nailer	-16
Billy Bob	7	Ashia	2
Nikolai	-48	Bhoomi	62
Daisy	39	Barbara	20
Captain	-20		

Fast Facts

Age: 17	
Home: Japan	
Likes: Disco, Thrills	
Dislikes: Observatory	
Special Needs: Entertainment	
Special Skills (Star Rating): Scavenging (1)	
Basic Skills: Repair, Pharmaceuticals, Electronics, Laser, Bio Research, Weeding, Power, Oxygen, Maintenance	
Walking Speed: Fast	

Profile

Aside from making quite different fashion statements, Kita and Hoshi are practically indistinguishable, as well as inseparable. Check out their stats. Every value in every table is exactly the same, plus or minus one point. So this profile of Kita could be read verbatim from everything previously said about Hoshi.

In fact, now that we think of it...

Basic/Special Needs

See Hoshi.

Entertainment

See Hoshi.

Other Notable Attributes

See Hoshi.

2-27. Like Hoshi, Kita gets the most fun at the Disco.

Relationships

See Hoshi.

2-28. Like Hoshi, Kita dislikes workout equipment.

Taking Kita's Pulse

Here's a look at how quickly Kita's six specific Need bars drop. The numbers represent how many units of game-time before the next "pulse" occurs for that Need bar. Each "pulse" lowers Kita's Need bar a fraction. Thus, the lower the number, the faster the bar goes down. A zero (0) means the character has no need in this category.

Need Bar for:	Time Between Downward Pulses
Money	200
Entertainment	400
Human Contact	50
Food	400
Hygiene	400
Sleep	200

(Lower number = Need Bar drops faster)

ENTERTAINMENT NEEDS: KITA

Activity	Entertainment Satisfaction Provided
Exercise	-2
Thrill	6
Combat Arena	1
Bar	0
Luxury Bar	0
Meditation Room	0
Library/Trainer	0
Piano	0
Relaxation Pod	0
Disco	10
Restaurant	0
Sauna	2
Jacuzzi	2
Observatory	0
Viewing Platform	0
Golf	2
Zoo Exhibit	0
Virtual Shop	4
Slot Machine	0

Entertainment Needs

A positive number for an activity means the Entertainment bar moves up. A negative number means the bar moves down. Zero (0) means the bar doesn't move at all in either direction.

Exercise = Rowing/Running Machines, Stairclimber

Thrill = Virtuality Chair, Zero-Gravity Playroom

Miscellaneous Attributes

Attribute	Rating	Attribute	Rating
Intelligence (0-10)	6	Happiness Boost from Pets (0-5)	0
(Higher number = Learns faster at Library or Trainer)		Litter Drop Rate (0-6)	2
Chance of Insanity (0 or 1-10)	2	(Higher number = Dirtier)	
(Higher number = Greater chance of going insane)		Rubbish Tolerance (0-5)	2
Greenery Benefit (0-10)	2	(Higher number = More intolerant)	
(Higher number = More satisfaction derived from plants)		Response to Counseling (1-10)	1
Noise Tolerance (0-5)	0	(Higher number = Faster back to sanity)	
(Higher number = More intolerant)		Response to Detention Center (1-10)	10
Expected Salary (0-6)	3	(Higher number = Faster back to sanity)	
(Higher number = Values money more)			

Basic Relationships

The following table lists Kita's starting relationship with each of the other 19 operatives in *Space Colony*. A positive number means the relationship is in the Friend range, with the highest possible friendship being 100. A negative number is in the Enemy range, with the deepest interpersonal loathing at -100. A relationship cannot drop any further than 50 points from the starting value listed in the table. However, it can rise clear up to 100 if properly nurtured.

Relationship with:	Rating
Venus	-2
Stig	-33
Tami	-64
Slim	-15
Dean	-26
Candy	7
Billy Bob	8
Nikolai	-49
Daisy	40
Captain	-21
Vasilios	-12
Kita	100
Mr. Zhang	-75
Greg	-38
Babette	-22
Nailer	-17
Ashia	3
Bhoomi	63
Barbara	21

Nailer McBride

Fast Facts

Age: 43	
Home: Scotland	
Likes: Combat Arena, Bar	
Dislikes: Piano	
Special Needs: Food, Sleep	
Special Skills (Star Rating): Weeding (3)	
Basic Skills: Mining, Repair, Cleaning, Maintenance	
Walking Speed: Average	

Profile

Nailer is a crude, aggressive sort of guy with a mean streak. Perfect for base synergy! He brings a very useful 3-star Weeding skill to the colony... but unfortunately, Nailer sometimes makes little distinction between pests and tourists. His basic skills are useful, too.

Basic/Special Needs

Nailer has never been one to postpone gratification. Most of his needs drop faster than normal, especially Food, which keeps him frequently seeking meals. Nailer needs a little extra Entertainment, Human Contact, and Sleep, too. Because both Food and Sleep are also special needs, Nailer is probably more in danger of becoming surly and unhappy (and then losing his mind) than any other colonist in the game.

2-29. Put Nailer to work outside at the Weeding Post, where his skills are best suited.

Entertainment

For Nailer, nothing says fun like the Combat Arena. Pounding virtual foes into virtual pulp brings him a satisfaction of 10, the highest possible. Not far behind is a trip to the Bar—but *not* the Luxury Bar, which is for snobs and bluehairs. Exercise and Thrill facilities give him an Entertainment boost, too.

Other Notable Attributes

When unhappy, Nailer has the highest chance of going insane in the game. When he does wig out, send him directly to the Detention Center for quick rehab. (Counseling is 10 times less efficient in restoring Nailer's sanity.) Nailer is not the brightest fellow, so teaching him new skills in the Library is extremely time consuming. Better to keep him manning the Weeding Post, where he's quite skillful.

2-30. Nailer's favorite pastime, by far, is virtual fighting in the Combat Arena.

Relationships

Nailer rubs a lot of people the wrong way, but for some reason he and Billy Bob really hit it off famously. He gets along fairly well with Bhoomi and Barbara, too; both start off high enough that they'll never become his enemy. On the other hand, his instant-enemies list is long, starting with Slim (by far the most negative rating), then Greg, Venus, and numerous others.

Taking Nailer's Pulse

Here's a look at how quickly Nailer's six specific Need bars drop. The numbers represent how many units of game-time before the next "pulse" occurs for that Need bar. Each "pulse" lowers Nailer's Need bar a fraction. Thus, the lower the number, the faster the bar goes down. A zero (0) means the character has no need in this category.

Need Bar for:	Time Between Downward Pulses
Money	200
Entertainment	100
Human Contact	100
Food	50
Hygiene	200
Sleep	100

(Lower number = Need Bar drops faster)

ENTERTAINMENT NEEDS: NAILER

Activity	Entertainment Satisfaction Provided
Exercise	5
Thrill	5
Combat Arena	10
Bar	7
Luxury Bar	1
Meditation Room	0
Library/Trainer	2
Piano	0
Relaxation Pod	0
Disco	1
Restaurant	0
Sauna	2
Jacuzzi	2
Observatory	0
Viewing Platform	0
Golf	1
Zoo Exhibit	0
Virtual Shop	0
Slot Machine	0

Entertainment Needs

A positive number for an activity means the Entertainment bar moves up. A negative number means the bar moves down. Zero (0) means the bar doesn't move at all in either direction.

Exercise = Rowing/Running Machines, Stairclimber

Thrill = Virtuality Chair, Zero-Gravity Playroom

Miscellaneous Attributes

Attribute	Rating
Intelligence (0-10)	2
(Higher number = Learns faster at Library or Trainer)	
Chance of Insanity (0 or 1-10)	10
(Higher number = Greater chance of going insane)	
Greenery Benefit (0-10)	0
(Higher number = More satisfaction derived from plants)	
Noise Tolerance (0-5)	0
(Higher number = More intolerant)	
Expected Salary (0-6)	1
(Higher number = Values money more)	

Attribute	Rating
Happiness Boost from Pets (0-5)	0
Litter Drop Rate (0-6)	3
(Higher number = Dirtier)	
Rubbish Tolerance (0-5)	0
(Higher number = More intolerant)	
Response to Counseling (1-10)	1
(Higher number = Faster back to sanity)	
Response to Detention Center (1-10)	10
(Higher number = Faster back to sanity)	

Basic Relationships

The following table lists Nailer's starting relationship with each of the other 19 operatives in *Space Colony*. A positive number means the relationship is in the Friend range, with the highest possible friendship being 100. A negative number is in the Enemy range, with the deepest interpersonal loathing at -100. A relationship cannot drop any further than 50 points from the starting value listed in the table. However, it can rise clear up to 100 if properly nurtured.

Relationship with:	Rating
Venus	-25
Stig	-16
Tami	-7
Slim	-68
Dean	-19
Candy	-10
Billy Bob	81
Nikolai	4
Daisy	20
Captain	-14
Vasilios	25
Hoshi	-16
Kita	-17
Mr. Zhang	18
Greg	-39
Babette	30
Ashia	17
Bhoomi	57
Barbara	55

Nikolai Volkov

Fast Facts

Age: 37	
Home: Ukraine	
Likes: Learning, Gambling, Observatory	
Dislikes: Shopping	
Special Needs: None	
Special Skills (Star Rating): Pharmaceuticals (2), Electronics (2), Bio Research (2), Scavenging (1), Cybernetics (1), Power (1), Oxygen (1)	
Basic Skills: None	
Walking Speed: Fast (1)	

Profile

If you can ignore his spastic Disco dancing (which isn't easy to do), Nikolai is a true colony treasure. His highly developed skill set includes 2-star ratings in Pharmaceuticals, Electronics, and Bio Research. In fact, *all* of his skills are above basic level. So Nikolai is a very valuable employee. He moves quickly from one task to the next, and he does a good job.

Basic/Special Needs

Nikolai has no special or fast-dropping needs. In fact, his needs for Sleep and Hygiene are low, while his other needs are no worse than normal. So he's relatively easy to manage.

Entertainment

Nikolai's high energy and a rabid intellectual curiosity could make it hard to find suitable Entertainment activities. Fortunately, if the Library is open, that's all Nikolai needs. Learning gives him the highest possible satisfaction of 10. Calculating the probabilities at play in a Slot Machine fascinates him, too, and his love of science extends to the Observatory.

2-31. Nikolai starts with a stunning array of high-level skills.

And then... well, there's always the Disco, if you can stand to watch him gyrate. But don't send him shopping. Nikolai finds the online search for and purchase of consumable items most distasteful.

2-32. Learning in the Library provides Nikolai intense pleasure.

Other Notable Attributes

The young Ukrainian has no special needs that require special attention. He is very, very smart—only Mr. Zhang is smarter. But high intelligence often puts one at risk for mental illness, and that is true here. Properly managed, Nikolai will rarely fall into the unhappiness that triggers episodes of insanity. But when he does, the chances of madness are high.

Relationships

Nikolai is difficult to dislike, but Hoshi and Kita manage to pull it off. Daisy finds his pointy-headed energy a little hard to take at first, too. But most everyone else starts in positive territory with Nikolai, especially Mr. Zhang and Bhoomi, his friends for life.

Taking Nikolai's Pulse

Here's a look at how quickly Nikolai's six specific Need bars drop. The numbers represent how many units of game-time before the next "pulse" occurs for that Need bar. Each "pulse" lowers Nikolai's Need bar a fraction. Thus, the lower the number, the faster the bar goes down. A zero (0) means the character has no need in this category.

Need Bar for:	Time Between Downward Pulses
Money	200
Entertainment	200
Human Contact	200
Food	200
Hygiene	500
Sleep	400

(Lower number = Need Bar drops faster)

Entertainment Needs

A positive number for an activity means the Entertainment bar moves up. A negative number means the bar moves down. Zero (0) means the bar doesn't move at all in either direction.

ENTERTAINMENT NEEDS: NIKOLAI

Activity	Entertainment Satisfaction Provided
Exercise	0
Thrill	0
Combat Arena	0
Bar	0
Luxury Bar	0
Meditation Room	0
Library/Trainer	10
Piano	1
Relaxation Pod	0
Disco	4
Restaurant	0
Sauna	0
Jacuzzi	0
Observatory	6
Viewing Platform	0
Golf	0
Zoo Exhibit	0
Virtual Shop	-10
Slot Machine	8

Exercise = Rowing/Running Machines, Stairclimber
Thrill = Virtuality Chair, Zero-Gravity Playroom

Basic Relationships

The following table lists Nikolai's starting relationship with each of the other 19 operatives in *Space Colony*. A positive number means the relationship is in the Friend range, with the highest possible friendship being 100. A negative number is in the Enemy range, with the deepest interpersonal loathing at -100. A relationship cannot drop any further than 50 points from the starting value listed in the table. However, it can rise clear up to 100 if properly nurtured.

NIKOLAI'S STARTING RELATIONSHIPS

Relationship with:	Rating
Venus	36
Stig	7
Tami	8
Slim	39
Dean	10
Candy	21
Billy Bob	42
Daisy	-10
Captain	38
Vasilios	17
Hoshi	-48
Kita	-49
Mr. Zhang	70
Greg	13
Babette	17
Nailer	4
Ashia	18
Bhoomi	61
Barbara	6

Miscellaneous Attributes

Attribute	Rating
Intelligence (0-10)	9
(Higher number = Learns faster at Library or Trainer)	
Chance of Insanity (0 or 1-10)	8
(Higher number = Greater chance of going insane)	
Greenery Benefit (0-10)	2
(Higher number = More satisfaction derived from plants)	
Noise Tolerance (0-5)	3
(Higher number = More intolerant)	
Expected Salary (0-6)	3
(Higher number = Values money more)	
Happiness Boost from Pets (0-5)	3
Litter Drop Rate (0-6)	3
(Higher number = Dirtier)	
Rubbish Tolerance (0-5)	1
(Higher number = More intolerant)	
Response to Counseling (1-10)	4
(Higher number = Faster back to sanity)	
Response to Detention Center (1-10)	4
(Higher number = Faster back to sanity)	

Fast Facts

Age: 15
Home: United States (New York)
Likes: Disco, Thrills, Jacuzzi
Dislikes: Golf, Exercise
Special Needs: Entertainment, Food
Special Skills (Star Rating): Laser (2)
Basic Skills: Weeding, Oxygen
Walking Speed: Average (2)

Profile

Slim is a typical teenage adolescent in most respects. "Brim full of attitude" is how Venus describes him, and he is, indeed, a punk by nature. However, unlike most punks, he is willing to work a little, and he brings a 2-star skill with Lasers to your base. Slim can also work backup at the Weeding Post or Oxygen console when he first steps off the shuttle.

Basic/Special Needs

Slim has a voracious need for entertainment. In fact, his Entertainment Need bar drops eight times faster than the average! On the other hand, his Hygiene Need is off the charts in the other direction. Slim very rarely needs a trip to the Personal Hygiene Pod. So skip Slim's showers and send him directly to his favorite Entertainment haunts instead.

Note also that Slim is one of those rare, difficult types with *two* special needs—in his case, Entertainment and Sleep. You know about his need for Entertainment, but Slim's Sleep bar drops a bit faster than normal, too. So you'll sometimes have your hands full trying to keep Slim's overall Happiness high.

2-33. Slim loves to break dance across the Disco floor.

Entertainment

Like the other base teens, Hoshi and Kita, Slim has a love/hate attitude toward physical exertion. He despises formal workouts on the exercise equipment, yet he gains the highest satisfaction of 10 from sweating and spinning on the Disco floor. Don't put him on a golf course, however. In Slim's estimation, nothing could be more pathetic than Golf.

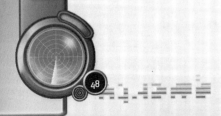

Naturally, Slim also gets high satisfaction from Thrill activities like the Virtuality Chair and Zero Gravity Playroom. He likes the Jacuzzi and Bar, too. (No drinking age cutoff in space, apparently.) Oddly enough, he finds learning fun, too. Put him in the Library to learn a new skill *and* be entertained, thus killing two Burnflies with one stone.

Other Notable Attributes

Slim is the biggest slob in the colony. He has the highest possible litter dropping rate, and he couldn't care less about rubbish, noise, or lack of greenery.

2-34. Slim really, really hates Golf. But he actually enjoys learning new stuff in the Library.

Relationships

Slim understandably annoys a lot of people, particularly Nailer, Daisy, Billy Bob, and Venus. But he starts out on very good terms with Stig and Bhoomi. Slim can easily remain friendly with Candy, too, with only minor maintenance.

Taking Slim's Pulse

Here's a look at how quickly Slim's six specific Need bars drop. The numbers represent how many units of game-time before the next "pulse" occurs for that Need bar. Each pulse lowers Slim's Need bar a fraction. Thus, the lower the number, the faster the bar goes down. A zero (0) means the character has no need in this category.

> Although the scale for pulse normally tops out at 1000, Slim's Hygiene pulse is 2000. He is a teenage, after all!

Need Bar for:	Time Between Downward Pulses
Money	200
Entertainment	25
Human Contact	200
Food	300
Hygiene	2000 (not a typo!)
Sleep	100

(Lower number = Need Bar drops faster)

Entertainment Needs

A positive number for an activity means the Entertainment bar moves up. A negative number means the bar moves down. Zero (0) means the bar doesn't move at all in either direction.

ENTERTAINMENT NEEDS: SLIM

Activity	Entertainment Satisfaction Provided
Exercise	-4
Thrill	8
Combat Arena	0
Bar	7
Luxury Bar	1
Meditation Room	0
Library/Trainer	5
Piano	0
Relaxation Pod	3
Disco	10
Restaurant	0
Sauna	0
Jacuzzi	7
Observatory	0
Viewing Platform	0
Golf	-10
Zoo Exhibit	0
Virtual Shop	2
Slot Machine	0

> Exercise = Rowing/Running Machines, Stairclimber
> Thrill = Virtuality Chair, Zero-Gravity Playroom

Miscellaneous Attributes

Attribute	Rating
Intelligence (0-10)	4
(Higher number = Learns faster at Library or Trainer)	
Chance of Insanity (0 or 1-10)	6
(Higher number = Greater chance of going insane)	
Greenery Benefit (0-10)	0
(Higher number = More satisfaction derived from plants)	
Noise Tolerance (0-5)	0
(Higher number = More intolerant)	
Expected Salary (0-6)	2
(Higher number = Values money more)	
Happiness Boost from Pets (0-5)	0
Litter Drop Rate (0-6)	6
(Higher number = Dirtier)	
Rubbish Tolerance (0-5)	0
(Higher number = More intolerant)	
Response to Counseling (1-10)	8
(Higher number = Faster back to sanity)	
Response to Detention Center (1-10)	8
(Higher number = Faster back to sanity)	

Basic Relationships

The following table lists Slim's starting relationship with each of the other 19 operatives in *Space Colony*. A positive number means the relationship is in the Friend range, with the highest possible friendship being 100. A negative number is in the Enemy range, with the deepest interpersonal loathing at -100. A relationship cannot drop any further than 50 points from the starting value listed in the table. However, it can rise clear up to 100 if properly nurtured.

SLIM'S STARTING RELATIONSHIPS

Relationship with:	Rating	Relationship with:	Rating
Venus	-43	Hoshi	-14
Stig	74	Kita	-15
Tami	10	Mr. Zhang	6
Dean	-21	Greg	-39
Candy	49	Babette	-13
Billy Bob	-43	Nailer	-68
Nikolai	-39	Ashia	-14
Daisy	-46	Bhoomi	64
Captain	-34	Barbara	2
Vasilios	13		

Stig Svensson

Fast Facts

Age: 36	
Home: Norway	
Likes: Sauna, Bar, Thrills	
Dislikes: Tami	
Special Needs: Food	
Special Skills (Star Rating): Mining (3), Repair (1), Laser (1), Power (1), Maintenance (1)	
Basic Skills: Nutrient Extraction, Space Gas, Electronics, Weeding, Oxygen, Cleaning	
Walking Speed: Average	

Profile

Stig is a jack of all trades and, amazingly enough, master of several. In particular, he's a 3-star Mining expert, just the man you want out on the planetary surface running your rigs. He also features above-basic skill at Repair and Maintenance, Laser operation, and Power console control. Indeed, Stig walks off the shuttle and into your base with 11 different skills. Other than Venus, Stig is your most-skilled colonist in the early going.

Basic/Special Needs

Of course, all that heavy labor in mining operations can give a man a powerful hunger. And Stig is no little fellow—he needs a *lot* of food to stay happy and working hard. Food is also a special need, so it causes more Unhappiness as it drops. So keep him well fed. Otherwise, Stig's needs are quite manageable. In fact, he requires less Sleep and Personal Hygiene attention than the average colonist.

Entertainment

For fun, Stig is a glutton for thrills, so send him to the Virtuality Chair or Zero-Gravity Playroom. He really likes his beer, too, so let Stig entertain himself at the local Bar.

2-35. Stig gets his biggest kicks out of thrill-oriented fun like the Zero Gravity Playroom.

(Like Nailer, he's not comfortable in the pretentious Luxury Bar, however.) Oddly, his Nordic physiology responds quite favorably to Sauna sessions. And what biker dude wouldn't find the Combat Arena a hoot?

Other Notable Attributes

Stig doesn't mind noise or rubbish, and he doesn't care at all about plants. But if he loses his mind, send him to the Detention Center rather than the Counseling Robot.

Relationships

Stig and Slim get along great, and Stig is solid friends with Venus, Charles, and Billy Bob, too. But when his hunger is high and his tolerance for Human Contact goes down, Stig can get punchy. In particular, keep him away from Tami if both are cranky. The possibly violent conflict will knock (literally) someone's Health bar right down into the red. Stig starts off quite negatively with Daisy and Babette, too. Nurture these relationships carefully.

2-36. Stig can get pushy with his enemies.

Taking Stig's Pulse

Here's a look at how quickly Stig's six specific Need bars drop. The numbers represent how many units of game-time before the next "pulse" occurs for that Need bar. Each "pulse" lowers Stig's Need bar a fraction Thus, the lower the number, the faster the bar goes down. A zero (0) means the character has no need in this category.

Need Bar for:	Time Between Downward Pulses
Money	200
Entertainment	200
Human Contact	200
Food	50
Hygiene	500
Sleep	400

(Lower number = Need Bar drops faster)

Entertainment Needs

A positive number for an activity means the Entertainment bar moves up. A negative number means the bar moves down. Zero (0) means the bar doesn't move at all in either direction.

> Exercise = Rowing/Running Machines, Stairclimber
> Thrill = Virtuality Chair, Zero-Gravity Playroom

Activity	Entertainment Satisfaction Provided
Exercise	1
Thrill	10
Combat Arena	6
Bar	8
Luxury Bar	0
Meditation Room	0
Library/Trainer	0
Piano	0
Relaxation Pod	2
Disco	4
Restaurant	0
Sauna	7
Jacuzzi	3
Observatory	0
Viewing Platform	0
Golf	0
Zoo Exhibit	0
Virtual Shop	3
Slot Machine	0

Miscellaneous Attributes

Attribute	Rating
Intelligence (0-10)	4
(Higher number = Learns faster at Library or Trainer)	
Chance of Insanity (0 or 1-10)	4
(Higher number = Greater chance of going insane)	
Greenery Benefit (0-10)	0
(Higher number = More satisfaction derived from plants)	
Noise Tolerance (0-5)	0
(Higher number = More intolerant)	
Expected Salary (0-6)	4
(Higher number = Values money more)	
Happiness Boost from Pets (0-5)	0
Litter Drop Rate (0-6)	3
(Higher number = Dirtier)	
Rubbish Tolerance (0-5)	0
(Higher number = More intolerant)	
Response to Counseling (1-10)	2
(Higher number = Faster back to sanity)	
Response to Detention Center (1-10)	10
(Higher number = Faster back to sanity)	

Basic Relationships

The following table lists Stig's starting relationship with each of the other 19 operatives in *Space Colony*. A positive number means the relationship is in the Friend range, with the highest possible friendship being 100. A negative number is in the Enemy range, with the deepest interpersonal loathing at -100. A relationship cannot drop any further than 50 points from the starting value listed in the table. However, it can rise clear up to 100 if properly nurtured.

STIG'S STARTING RELATIONSHIPS

Relationship with:	Rating	Relationship with:	Rating
Venus	61	Hoshi	-32
Tami	-71	Kita	-33
Slim	74	Mr. Zhang	54
Dean	32	Greg	-37
Candy	17	Babette	-51
Billy Bob	41	Nailer	-16
Nikolai	7	Ashia	12
Daisy	-64	Bhoomi	42
Captain	62	Barbara	-40
Vasilios	-11		

Fast Facts

Age: 42	
Home: United States (Texas)	
Likes: Bar, Luxury Bar	
Dislikes: Exercise	
Special Needs: Human Contact	
Special Skills (Star Rating): Cleaning (2)	
Basic Skills: Power, Oxygen	
Walking Speed: Slow	

Profile

Tami La Belle's a real piece of work. She's crusty, cranky, needy, and she swings a frightening left hook. Her desire for Human Contact can be smothering and disruptive. She hates to work and loves to booze, big time. Yet someone with 2 stars of Cleaning skill is always welcome in *Space Colony*. She pushes a broom with delicate expertise. And her backup basic skills in Power and Oxygen really help in the early campaign missions, when your colony population is still just three or four people.

Basic/Special Needs

Tami's Hygiene need is very low, so she can forgo showers in favor of the Human Contact that she so desperately needs. This relentless (and special) need for Human Contact can be tough to satisfy at times, especially if an emergency hits the base or you're rushing to beat a time limit. One answer: Install a Counseling Robot—preferably halfway between Tami's Cleaning Post and the nearest Bar—and send her there regularly.

Entertainment

When it comes to entertainment, Tami has some intense likes and dislikes. She derives the highest possible satisfaction in a Bar or Luxury Bar. (Fancy or not doesn't matter—just so long as the bartendroid pours a good stiff shot.) She's also fond of the Slot Machine and Relaxation Pod, and enjoys a little line dancing at the Disco.

2-37. Tami loves to belly up to the Bar.

2-38. Exercise is Tami's least favorite activity. Not to mention it's a bit disturbing to watch...

But Tami hates learning at the Library. She also hates Golf and thrill-based entertainment like the Virtuality Chair and Zero-Gravity Playroom. Worst of all, Tami absolutely loathes exercise of any kind. Do not put this woman on a Running Machine. It's not a pretty sight, man.

Other Notable Attributes

Tami has no use for plants; as far as she's concerned, they belong outside, or on a salad plate. Her salary expectation is low, along with her intelligence level.

Relationships

Tami starts with high animosity toward Stig, Hoshi, and Kita. She has other enemies, too; Dean, Daisy, and Babette are dang fools in her book. Only Greg and Bhoomi are Tami's guaranteed friends.

Taking Tami's Pulse

Here's a look at how quickly Tami's six specific Need bars drop. The numbers represent how many units of game-time before the next "pulse" occurs for that Need bar. Each "pulse" lowers Tami's Need bar a fraction. Thus, the lower the number, the faster the bar goes down. A zero (0) means the character has no need in this category.

Need Bar for:	Time Between Downward Pulses
Money	200
Entertainment	200
Human Contact	25
Food	200
Hygiene	600
Sleep	200

(Lower number = Need Bar drops faster)

Entertainment Needs

A positive number for an activity means the Entertainment bar moves up. A negative number means the bar moves down. Zero (0) means the bar doesn't move at all in either direction.

ENTERTAINMENT NEEDS: TAMI

Activity	Entertainment Satisfaction Provided
Exercise	-8
Thrill	-2
Combat Arena	0
Bar	10
Luxury Bar	10
Meditation Room	0
Library/Trainer	-2
Piano	0
Relaxation Pod	5
Disco	4
Restaurant	0
Sauna	3
Jacuzzi	3
Observatory	0
Viewing Platform	0
Golf	-4
Zoo Exhibit	4
Virtual Shop	4
Slot Machine	5

Exercise = Rowing/Running Machines, Stairclimber
Thrill = Virtuality Chair, Zero-Gravity Playroom

Miscellaneous Attributes

Attribute	Rating
Intelligence (0-10)	2
(Higher number = Learns faster at Library or Trainer)	
Chance of Insanity (0 or 1-10)	2
(Higher number = Greater chance of going insane)	
Greenery Benefit (0-10)	0
(Higher number = More satisfaction derived from plants)	
Noise Tolerance (0-5)	1
(Higher number = More intolerant)	
Expected Salary (0-6)	2
(Higher number = Values money more)	
Happiness Boost from Pets (0-5)	1
Litter Drop Rate (0-6)	1
(Higher number = Dirtier)	
Rubbish Tolerance (0-5)	1
(Higher number = More intolerant)	
Response to Counseling (1-10)	6
(Higher number = Faster back to sanity)	
Response to Detention Center (1-10)	8
(Higher number = Faster back to sanity)	

Basic Relationships

The following table lists Tami's starting relationship with each of the other 19 operatives in *Space Colony*. A positive number means the relationship is in the Friend range, with the highest possible friendship being 100. A negative number is in the Enemy range, with the deepest interpersonal loathing at -100. A relationship cannot drop any further than 50 points from the starting value listed in the table. However, it can rise clear up to 100 if properly nurtured.

TAMI'S STARTING RELATIONSHIPS

Relationship with:	Rating	Relationship with:	Rating
Venus	10	Hoshi	-63
Stig	-71	Kita	-64
Slim	10	Mr. Zhang	25
Dean	-43	Greg	64
Candy	-18	Babette	-32
Billy Bob	12	Nailer	-7
Nikolai	8	Ashia	-13
Daisy	-35	Bhoomi	63
Captain	33	Barbara	-11
Vasilios	22		

Vasilios Robot Cosmos

Fast Facts

Age: 30	
Home: Greece	
Likes: Observatory	
Special Needs: None	
Special Skills (Star Rating): None	
Basic Skills: Mining, Nutrient Extraction, Repair, Space Gas, Weeding, Power, Oxygen, Cleaning, Maintenance	
Walking Speed: Average	

Profile

This is one weird cat. Vasilios has no special skills or needs, and displays an extremely odd sensibility. He walks around saying things like: "I have no frame of reference. This is new to me. I remember... nothing." He's from Greece, but we don't think that quite explains it. Vasilios does have a good set of basic skills, however—nine of them, to be exact—and he works conscientiously when you assign him jobs. His answer to almost every directive you give him is "Okay."

Basic/Special Needs

The man needs almost nothing badly. His money needs are normal (strangely enough), but every other need drops four times slower than normal. Indeed, you can often ignore Vasilios for long periods of time without losing him to Unhappiness and the possibility of insanity.

Entertainment

Vasilios finds nothing particularly entertaining... except for stargazing in the Observatory, which he seems to love to the point of obsession. In fact, the Observatory gives Vasilios the highest possible satisfaction—the *only* satisfaction. Everything else does absolutely nothing for his Entertainment Need.

2-39. Vasilios finds only one activity entertaining, but it gets a 10—stargazing at the Observatory.

2-40. Vasilios is an excellent worker because his Need bars (including Food, Sleep, and Hygiene) drop so slowly.

Other Notable Attributes

Vasilios is smart and learns new skills quickly. He also finds plant life very soothing. His chance of madness is high if he grows unhappy, and once he loses his mind, he requires a long stint in either the Detention Center or with the Counseling Robot to recover his wits.

Relationships

Daisy and Bhoomi have very good relationships with the Greek space cadet. Other than Mr. Zhang, few colonists really dislike him much. He starts out negative with just three other people—Hoshi, Kita, and Stig.

Taking Vasilios's Pulse

Here's a look at how quickly Vasilios's six specific Need bars drop. The numbers represent how many units of game-time before the next "pulse" occurs for that Need bar. Each "pulse" lowers Vasilios's Need bar a fraction. Thus, the lower the number, the faster the bar goes down. A zero (0) means the character has no need in this category.

Need Bar for:	Time Between Downward Pulses
Money	200
Entertainment	800
Human Contact	800
Food	800
Hygiene	800
Sleep	800

(Lower number = Need Bar drops faster)

Entertainment Needs

A positive number for an activity means the Entertainment bar moves up. A negative number means the bar moves down. Zero (0) means the bar doesn't move at all in either direction.

ENTERTAINMENT NEEDS: VASILIOS

Activity	Entertainment Satisfaction Provided
Exercise	0
Thrill	0
Combat Arena	0
Bar	0
Luxury Bar	0
Meditation Room	0
Library/Trainer	0
Piano	0
Relaxation Pod	0
Disco	0
Restaurant	0
Sauna	0
Jacuzzi	0
Observatory	10
Viewing Platform	0
Golf	0
Zoo Exhibit	0
Virtual Shop	0
Slot Machine	0

Exercise = Rowing/Running Machines, Stairclimber
Thrill = Virtuality Chair, Zero-Gravity Playroom

Miscellaneous Attributes

Attribute	Rating
Intelligence (0-10)	7
(Higher number = Learns faster at Library or Trainer)	
Chance of Insanity (0 or 1-10)	7
(Higher number = Greater chance of going insane)	
Greenery Benefit (0-10)	8
(Higher number = More satisfaction derived from plants)	
Noise Tolerance (0-5)	0
(Higher number = More intolerant)	
Expected Salary (0-6)	1
(Higher number = Values money more)	
Happiness Boost from Pets (0-5)	0
Litter Drop Rate (0-6)	0
(Higher number = Dirtier)	
Rubbish Tolerance (0-5)	0
(Higher number = More intolerant)	
Response to Counseling (1-10)	1
(Higher number = Faster back to sanity)	
Response to Detention Center (1-10)	1
(Higher number = Faster back to sanity)	

Basic Relationships

The following table lists Vasilios's starting relationship with each of the other 19 operatives in *Space Colony*. A positive number means the relationship is in the Friend range, with the highest possible friendship being 100. A negative number is in the Enemy range, with the deepest interpersonal loathing at -100. A relationship cannot drop any further than 50 points from the starting value listed in the table. However, it can rise clear up to 100 if properly nurtured.

Relationship with:	Rating
Venus	10
Stig	-11
Tami	22
Slim	13
Dean	14
Candy	25
Billy Bob	46
Nikolai	17
Daisy	68
Captain	19
Hoshi	-11
Kita	-12
Mr. Zhang	-73
Greg	16
Babette	20
Nailer	25
Ashia	31
Bhoomi	61
Barbara	9

Venus Jones

Fast Facts

Age: 23	
Home: United States (Colorado)	
Likes: Exercise, Luxury Bar, Meditation Room	
Dislikes: Gambling	
Special Needs: None	
Special Skills (Star Rating): Nutrient Extraction (3), Power (2), Oxygen (2)	
Basic Skills: Mining, Repair, Space Gas, Scavenging, Industrial Robotics, Military Robotics, Laser, Weeding, Cleaning, Maintenance	
Walking Speed: Average	

Profile

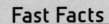

Venus is just a heck of a gal. The unspoken leader of the colony workforce, she has few, if any, personality flaws and plenty of special skills. A 3-star expert in Nutrient Extraction, Venus is also highly proficient in the colony's Power and Oxygen control systems. She adds basic skills in some of the more advanced technologies, such as Industrial and Military Robotics, and Space Gas (Argon) extraction methods.

Basic/Special Needs

Venus works hard and requires less Human Contact or Entertainment than most people. This makes her an easy character to manage, since those two needs are usually the most time-consuming to handle.

2-41. Venus is highly skilled in Nutrient Extraction, so put her in charge of your primary harvester.

Entertainment

Being from Colorado, Venus was raised in a culture of fitness and loves to exercise more than anything else. But hey, she's not a total health nut; she also enjoys hanging in the Luxury Bar for the wining, dining, and companionship. Venus also likes to use downtime to regain her equilibrium. The Relaxation Pod and Meditation Room are two of her favorite recreation spots.

2-42. Venus gets a positive jolt out of many activities, but her favorite is exercise.

The tomboy in her finds plenty of entertainment in the Combat Arena, as well, and she enjoys intense turns in the Virtuality Chair and Zero-Gravity Playroom. The Disco, Jacuzzi, and Sauna all have equal appeal. All in all, Venus is easily entertained and managed. She's definitely your go-to girl.

Other Notable Attributes

Venus is intelligent and a fast learner. She has high salary expectations, but nothing outrageous. She likes plants and pets well enough. And she has a zero-percent chance of losing her sanity when stressed out and unhappy.

Relationships

Greg, Barbara, and Slim get on her nerves. But she can always count on friendship from Billy Bob, Ashia, and her old buddy, Stig.

Taking Venus's Pulse

Here's a look at how quickly Venus's six specific Need bars drop. The numbers represent how many units of game-time before the next "pulse" occurs for that Need bar. Each "pulse" lowers Venus's Need bar a fraction. Thus, the lower the number, the faster the bar goes down. A zero (0) means the character has no need in this category.

Need Bar for:	Time Between Downward Pulses
Money	200
Entertainment	300
Human Contact	400
Food	300
Hygiene	200
Sleep	200

(Lower number = Need Bar drops faster)

ENTERTAINMENT NEEDS: VENUS

Activity	Entertainment Satisfaction Provided
Exercise	8
Thrill	3
Combat Arena	4
Bar	4
Luxury Bar	7
Meditation Room	6
Library/Trainer	0
Piano	0
Relaxation Pod	6
Disco	5
Restaurant	4
Sauna	5
Jacuzzi	5
Observatory	0
Viewing Platform	0
Golf	3
Zoo Exhibit	0
Virtual Shop	0
Slot Machine	0

Entertainment Needs

A positive number for an activity means the Entertainment bar moves up. A negative number means the bar moves down. Zero (0) means the bar doesn't move at all in either direction.

Exercise = Rowing/Running Machines, Stairclimber
Thrill = Virtuality Chair, Zero-Gravity Playroom

Miscellaneous Attributes

Attribute	Rating
Intelligence (0-10)	7
(Higher number = Learns faster at Library or Trainer)	
Chance of Insanity (0 or 1-10)	0
(Higher number = Greater chance of going insane)	
Greenery Benefit (0-10)	5
(Higher number = More satisfaction derived from plants)	
Noise Tolerance (0-5)	2
(Higher number = More intolerant)	
Expected Salary (0-6)	4
(Higher number = Values money more)	
Happiness Boost from Pets (0-5)	2
Litter Drop Rate (0-6)	0.4
(Higher number = Dirtier)	
Rubbish Tolerance (0-5)	2
(Higher number = More intolerant)	
Response to Counseling (1-10)	10
(Higher number = Faster back to sanity)	
Response to Detention Center (1-10)	5
(Higher number = Faster back to sanity)	

Basic Relationships

The following table lists Venus's starting relationship with each of the other 19 operatives in *Space Colony*. A positive number means the relationship is in the Friend range, with the highest possible friendship being 100. A negative number is in the Enemy range, with the deepest interpersonal loathing at -100. A relationship cannot drop any further than 50 points from the starting value listed in the table. However, it can rise clear up to 100 if properly nurtured.

VENUS'S STARTING RELATIONSHIPS

Relationship with:	Rating		Relationship with:	Rating
Stig	61		Hoshi	-1
Tami	10		Kita	-2
Slim	-43		Mr. Zhang	53
Dean	54		Greg	-66
Candy	46		Babette	-20
Billy Bob	75		Nailer	-25
Nikolai	36		Ashia	81
Daisy	43		Bhoomi	61
Captain	31		Barbara	-59
Vasilios	10			

Mr. Zhang

Fast Facts

Age: 80	
Home: China	
Likes: Sauna, Jacuzzi, Meditation Room	
Dislikes: Golf, Zoo Exhibit	
Special Needs: Sleep	
Special Skills (Star Rating): Cybernetics (4), Bio Research (2)	
Basic Skills: None	
Walking Speed: Very Slow	

Profile

Eighty year-old Mr. Zhang starts with only two skills, but his level of expertise in both is impressive. Venus calls him "the Cybernetics king," and he shuffles onto the scene with four stars of Cybernetics skill. But his Bio Research skill (two stars) isn't shabby, either. The Psychiatrist's Report calls him "a sour and begrudging old man," but Venus says he's really a nice guy underneath it all... and his stats prove her right.

2-43. Put Mr. Zhang to work in your Cybernetics Lab making android laborers for your colony.

Basic/Special Needs

Sleep. This, in a word, is Mr. Zhang's major drawback. His Sleep Need bar drops like a rock, so he requires some serious napping. Sleep is a special need for him, too, so unless you get him to bed regularly, his Happiness hovers in the yellow and red zones. Otherwise his needs are quite manageable. He requires less Food and Entertainment than the average colonist does.

Entertainment

Mr. Zhang finds the ultimate satisfaction in the purifying heat of the Sauna, with the Jacuzzi running a close second. He also enjoys meditation, exercise, and several other pursuits. Two phenomena absolutely irk him, however—Golf and Zoo Exhibits.

Other Notable Attributes

Mr. Zhang is the smartest person in the colony, bar none. If you need an emergency backup in a particular area that's lacking skilled workers, send the old fellow to the Library for a quick course of study. He learns fast! Mr. Zhang also has high salary expectations, so consider a bump in colony pay levels to keep him satisfied.

Relationships

The Psychiatrist may call him "sour," but Mr. Zhang actually starts off with very few enemies, most prominently Hoshi, Kita, and Vasilios. His permanent friends include Bhoomi, Nikolai, Stig, and Venus.

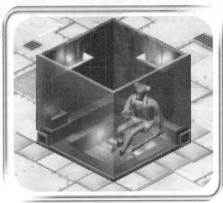

2-44. Nothing raises Mr. Zhang's spirits like a good sweat in the Sauna.

Taking Mr. Zhang's Pulse

Here's a look at how quickly Zhang's six specific Need bars drop. The numbers represent how many units of game-time before the next "pulse" occurs for that Need bar. Each "pulse" lowers Zhang's Need bar a fraction. Thus, the lower the number, the faster the bar goes down. A zero (0) means the character has no need in this category.

Need Bar for:	Time Between Downward Pulses
Money	200
Entertainment	400
Human Contact	200
Food	400
Hygiene	100
Sleep	25

(Lower number = Need Bar drops faster)

Entertainment Needs

A positive number for an activity means the Entertainment bar moves up. A negative number means the bar moves down. Zero (0) means the bar doesn't move at all in either direction.

ENTERTAINMENT NEEDS: MR. ZHANG

Activity	Entertainment Satisfaction Provided
Exercise	5
Thrill	3
Combat Arena	2
Bar	0
Luxury Bar	0
Meditation Room	6
Library/Trainer	0
Piano	4
Relaxation Pod	4
Disco	1
Restaurant	0
Sauna	10
Jacuzzi	8
Observatory	0
Viewing Platform	0
Golf	-10
Zoo Exhibit	-10
Virtual Shop	3
Slot Machine	4

Exercise = Rowing/Running Machines, Stairclimber
Thrill = Virtuality Chair, Zero-Gravity Playroom

Miscellaneous Attributes

Attribute	Rating
Intelligence (0-10)	10
(Higher number = Learns faster at Library or Trainer)	
Chance of Insanity (0 or 1-10)	1
(Higher number = Greater chance of going insane)	
Greenery Benefit (0-10)	4
(Higher number = More satisfaction derived from plants)	
Noise Tolerance (0-5)	3
(Higher number = More intolerant)	
Expected Salary (0-6)	5
(Higher number = Values money more)	
Happiness Boost from Pets (0-5)	3
Litter Drop Rate (0-6)	0
(Higher number = Dirtier)	
Rubbish Tolerance (0-5)	3
(Higher number = More intolerant)	
Response to Counseling (1-10)	2
(Higher number = Faster back to sanity)	
Response to Detention Center (1-10)	8
(Higher number = Faster back to sanity)	

Basic Relationships

The following table lists Mr. Zhang's starting relationship with each of the other 19 operatives in *Space Colony*. A positive number means the relationship is in the Friend range, with the highest possible friendship being 100. A negative number is in the Enemy range, with the deepest interpersonal loathing at -100. A relationship cannot drop any further than 50 points from the starting value listed in the table. However, it can rise clear up to 100 if properly nurtured.

MR. ZHANG'S STARTING RELATIONSHIPS

Relationship with:	Rating	Relationship with:	Rating
Venus	53	Vasilios	-73
Stig	54	Hoshi	-74
Tami	25	Kita	-75
Slim	6	Greg	-19
Dean	27	Babette	13
Candy	18	Nailer	18
Billy Bob	-19	Ashia	34
Nikolai	70	Bhoomi	74
Daisy	-21	Barbara	22
Captain	12		

TOURISTS

2-45. When a tourist shuttle unloads at your Tourist Port, your colony takes on a whole new character.

Four generic tourist types (Dad, Mom, Boy, Girl) begin to infest... er, visit your colony base once you install a Tourist Port. You have no control over these people, but they do have certain statistical characteristics you might find illuminating.

For example, tourist adults have very different ideas of fun than their kids do. Adults love Golf followed by a nice Sauna; kids hate both activities with a passion. Adults enjoy the bar scene; kids are bored to death by it. On the other hand, kids are thrill seekers who love the Virtuality Chair and Zero Gravity Playroom, while adults are less than enthused. Mom and the kids love the Disco; Dads are pretty lukewarm about dancing.

Look over these tables to see what's required for a 5-star tourist attraction.

Entertainment Needs

Tourists have very specific entertainment likes and dislikes. A positive number for an activity means the Entertainment bar moves up. A negative number means the bar moves down. Zero (0) means the bar doesn't move at all in either direction.

ENTERTAINMENT NEEDS: TOURISTS

Activity	Entertainment Satisfaction Provided			
	Dad	Mom	Boy	Girl
Exercise	8	5	-10	-10
Thrill	2	1	10	5
Combat Arena	5	6	6	7
Bar	9	3	-10	-10
Luxury Bar	6	8	-10	-10
Meditation Room	2	8	-10	4
Library/Trainer	-10	-10	-10	-10
Piano	4	6	7	10
Relaxation Pod	4	8	3	7
Disco	1	8	7	10
Restaurant	6	10	2	2
Sauna	6	9	-10	-10
Jacuzzi	5	10	3	10
Observatory	-10	-10	-10	-10
Viewing Platform	10	10	10	10
Golf	10	10	-10	-10
Zoo Exhibit	10	10	10	10
Virtual Shop	-10	-10	-10	-10
Slot Machine	4	1	-10	-10

Exercise = Rowing/Running Machines, Stairclimber
Thrill = Virtuality Chair, Zero-Gravity Playroom

Tourist Pulses

You can't see tourist Need bars... but just for the heck of it, here's a look at how quickly they drop for each of the four tourist types. Again, the numbers represent how many units of game-time before the next "pulse" occurs for that Need bar. Each "pulse" lowers the tourist's Need bar a fraction. Thus, the lower the number, the faster the bar goes down. A zero (0) means the tourist has no need in this category.

NEEDS PULSES: TOURISTS

Need Bar for:	Time Between Downward Pulses		
	Dad	Mom	Boy & Girl
Money	0	0	0
Entertainment	350	400	250
Human Contact	200	1000	1000
Food	350	400	250
Hygiene	1000	1000	1000
Sleep	1000	1000	1000

Some Fast Facts about Tourism

Here are a few tidbits of info to remember when you're constructing your tourist resort on Celensoan 4b:

- Tourists arrive only if you have a Tourist Port. You can place only one port on the planet.
- A tourist shuttle arrives once every four days.
- A tourist shuttle can deliver up to 40 tourists to your resort. The higher your Tourism Rating, the more tourists arrive... as long as you have the hotel space to accommodate them.
- The number of arriving tourists is limited by the number of hotel rooms available in your resort (up to a total of 40).
- Tourists check into their hotel and stay there for a few hours when they first arrive.
- Tourists stay four days, leaving when the next shuttle arrives.
- Tourists are totally autonomous, attending to their own needs. All you can do is provide facilities to entertain and feed them.
- The overall Tourism Rating is an average of the four categories of sub-ratings: Entertainment, Health & Hygiene, Food & Drink, and Safety. The more facilities you have that attend to a category (e.g., Medi Bays and showers to boost Health & Hygiene), the higher the tourist rating for that category.

CHAPTER 3
THE CATHERWOOD MISSIONS

3-1. Stig and Venus land on the planet Catherwood, home of some lovely lava pits and vicious Mutant Bees.

Catherwood is a bleak, forbidding world with enough raw materials to make a mining colony profitable for Blackwater Industries GC... and enough pests and discomforts to make life unpleasant for planetside colonists. You start with a skeleton staff of Venus, Stig, and Tami. By the final mission you have quite a motley crew of operatives.

Note that the first few Catherwood missions function as low-pressure learning exercises—kind of like tutorials, but undirected. Then things get hectic.

Ready? Here we go.

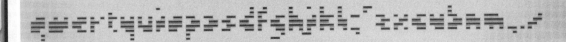

MISSION: *TAMI'S TRAINING*

Background

"Power and oxygen levels are to be raised to operational levels. Operative Tami is to re-acquaint herself with these controls. Nutrient stocks are to be established in readiness for base expansion."

Main Objectives

- Assign beds to all 3 colonists.
- Stockpile 5 units of base nutrients.
- Train Tami on Power Desk.

New Operatives

Name: Venus Jones

Mission Job: Nutrient Extraction
Backup Job: Oxygen or Power

Name: Tami La Belle

Mission Job: Power
Backup Job: Oxygen

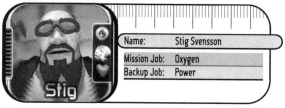

Name: Stig Svensson

Mission Job: Oxygen
Backup Job: Power

New Stuff Available

- Airlock
- Light
- Base Nutrients Extractor
- Plant
- Disco
- Solar Power Plant
- Bed
- Mess Hall

The Walkthrough

Again, the early missions are pretty easy if you understand the basic operation of a space colony. (You *did* read the manual, didn't you?) As the mission opens, the colony is activated. Your three colony "operatives"—Venus, Stig, and Tami—arrive via personnel shuttle at the base.

Make a Bedroom

You can complete the first mission objective before your colonists even shed their spacesuits. Click the Furniture button on the Building Selection Panel running down the left side of the screen. A menu of furniture items appears. Select "Bed" from the menu, then place one in a corner of the colony's Small Bio Dome.

Place each new bed as far into the corner of the Small Bio Dome as you can (see 3-2).
You can fit exactly four beds into a Small Bio Dome if you maximize the space.

Repeat twice more, placing a total of three beds in the Small Bio Dome.

Now you have a "bedroom" with beds for all three colonists. Creating dedicated bedrooms should be standard operating procedure when you need more beds for incoming operatives. Colonists sleep much better in rooms that have nothing but beds.

3-2. Use your Furniture menu to make your Small Bio Dome into a bedroom. Place beds in corners to maximize space.

Assign Beds

Left-click on Venus to select her, and then left-click on one of the beds. This assigns that bed to Venus, and its bedcover turns blue.

Now select Stig by left-clicking on the Stig icon in the lower-right corner of the screen. (Or you can just right-click anywhere to clear the cursor selection, and then left-click directly on Stig himself to select him.) When Stig is selected, left-click on one of the two other beds to assign it to your hulking Norwegian biker; his bedcover turns black with a white demon insignia.

Repeat this process with Tami, who gets a heart-emblazoned love bed. You get a nice spoken acknowledgment that a mission objective has been completed.
Objective completed.

3-3. Each colonist gets a distinctive bedcover to identify their bed once you assign it.

We'll refer to this first Small Bio Dome as your "bedroom" as we progress through the missions. You'll add more Small Bio Domes for bedrooms as you gain operatives.

Yes, that *was* ridiculously easy. But enjoy the leisurely pace while you can. Trust us, this Campaign is going to get much, much more hectic.

Raise Power and Oxygen Levels

The Mission Background suggested that you raise Power and Oxygen levels to operational status and re-acquaint "Operative Tami" with these controls. This is a good idea, since a space colony low on oxygen is not a particularly pleasant place to live.

3-4. Put Tami to work at the Power Console (circled). When she fires up the Solar Power Plants (upper-left), the Power Subsystem gauge rises.

Select Tami, then left-click the Power Console on the Bridge. (It's the center console, marked by the Power icon, a yellow bolt of electricity.) She tromps to work there; when she mans the console, your Solar Power Plants blossom open and your Power level rises quickly.
Objective completed.

You can check this by observing the gauge over the Power console or by clicking the "Go to Bridge" button in the lower-left corner, and then observing the yellow Power Subsystem gauge (see 3-4)—yep, Tami's got you powered up real good.

Now select Stig and click on the Oxygen Console to get him working there. (It's the rightmost console, marked by the Oxygen icon, white air bubbles on a blue background.) Again, you can see the Oxygen level rise by observing the gauge over the console or by clicking the "Go to Bridge" button and observing the blue Oxygen Subsystem gauge.

Who's Your Buddy?

Tami is particularly needy when it comes to Human Contact, but she despises Stig as the mission opens. In fact, chances are very good she'll punch Stig silly for no apparent reason before this mission is over. But Tami likes Venus—everybody likes Venus—so you can arrange interactions between the two to boost their Human Contact ratings.

3-5. Tami and Stig may "hit it off" in an all-too-literal manner. In fact, they'll see each other as enemies until you discover a way to encourage their friendship in the next mission.

3-6. Make "Small Talk" between Tami and Venus to satisfy their Human Contact Need. (Tami is very needy in this area.) Do the same with Stig and Venus.

Just select either female colonist, then click on the other woman to get the interaction icons. Click on the "Small Talk" icon (see 3-6) to bring the girls together for a quick chat.

Do the same with Stig and Venus. They get along fine, too. But try to keep Stig and Tami apart as much as possible...or else you'll have a medical emergency on your hands, sooner or later.

Flesh Out the Colony

Oxygen, power, beds, and small talk are good things. But man needs more to survive. Dancing, for example. A gal like Tami cannot thrive without stepping out every now and again. Stig, too, gets depressed without someplace to rock on air guitar. So click the "Recreation" button, select Disco, and place it in a corner of your Medium Bio Dome.

3-7. The Disco floor meets Entertainment Needs, while your Mess Hall provides the basic nutrients necessary for survival.

Food is next. Click the "Food and Drink" button and select the Mess Hall. Place it in another corner of your Medium Bio Dome. But note that nobody can actually *eat* here yet. The Mess Hall's tall converter-tube needs canisters of base nutrients that it can convert into simple food. Without these nutrients, no food.

Where does your Mess Hall get these nutrient canisters? Let's move on to the next step.

Acquire Base Nutrient Stocks

Your third official objective is to acquire resources for 5 units of base nutrients. Select a "Light" from your Engineering menu and place it to the right (east) of the colony base. See the ring of small red lights? Those are "operational zone markers"–boundary markers. Beyond them is the Forbidden Zone, where you cannot go (yet).

Now observe all those green, willowy plants. Move your cursor over them to get an info window–they're Hydromorphus plants, an excellent food source. But to get food, you need a Nutrient Extractor to harvest Hydromorphus and convert it into base nutrients.

Hydromorphus
Use the Nutrient Extractor to harvest this resource for food.

3-8. Place a Light to illuminate the east, then drop a Nutrient Extractor amongst the lush Hydromorphus plants.

Click the Industry button, select "Nutrient Extractor" (the only item on the menu right now), and then place the machinery amongst the Hydromorphus plants near the red lights. (You can't place *any* item unless you can see its full image where the cursor is. Keep moving the cursor until you see the image appear.)

Place your Nutrient Extractor as far to the east as you can find a spot. You need the space next to your Bio Domes in future missions.

Man the Extractor

The Extractor comes complete with a Nutrient Robot to do the harvesting. But you need a worker to run the system—preferably one with a high Nutrient Extraction skill rating. How do we find that?

Select Venus to bring up her Colonist Panel, then click on the brain icon next to her portrait to open her Skills window. Venus has a lot of ability–13 skills in all!–but her skill level is highest in Oxygen (2 stars), Power (2 stars), and by golly, Nutrient Extraction (3 stars).

3-9. Venus, with a 3-star skill rating, is easily your best nutrient extraction worker.

So send Venus to work harvesting nutrients. You already have her selected, so just left-click on the Nutrient Extractor you've placed. She cheerily goes to her new job, and soon the machine is producing a canister of extracted nutrient, which a warehouse droid promptly picks up and whisks over for insertion into your Mess Hall converter.

The droid deposits additional canisters in a storage tank in the

3-10. A warehouse droid stockpiles spare canisters of extracted nutrient in warehouse storage tanks.

3-11. Congratulations on your first baby step.

Warehouse next to the Shuttle Pad near the top of the screen. Once it delivers the fifth canister of base nutrients, the voice declares: "Mission success!"
Objective completed.

Good start. But hey—it's *just* a start.

MISSION: CLEANING UP

Background

"Final preparations before mission instructions arrive. Base cleanliness levels are low and are affecting staff morale. Use the cleaning stations provided to rectify this situation. Hygiene pods and social area facilities are now online and available for staff usage."

Main Objectives

- Clean up base litter.
- Raise Stig and Tami's relationship to Friends.

New Operatives

None—you have the same three colonists you started with: Venus, Tami, and Stig.

New Stuff Available

- Social Area
- Running Machine
- Cleaning Post
- Maintenance Post
- Hygiene Pod

The Walkthrough

If you review Venus' Diary in the Mission Briefing screen, you get some additional direction. Aside from getting your colonists and their base cleaned up, you need to pay special attention to the swiftly deteriorating relationship between Tami and Stig.

Clean Base, Clean People

Click the Engineering button, select a Cleaning Post (cost: 250 credits), and place it in an open corner of the Medium Bio Dome. Who should we put to work there? Hint: Check Tami's skills by clicking the brain icon on her Character window. She has only three skills, but at a 2-star skill level, Cleaning is her forte.

3-12. Your base is getting kind of skuzzy, but Tami is a 2-star Cleaning expert. Drop in a Cleaning Post for her.

Select Tami and left-click the Cleaning Post to assign that as her Primary Job. (This automatically moves Power to the Secondary Job slot on her Colonist Panel.)

Job Shift

What about the Power desk, you ask? Note that Stig has a one-star skill rating in Power, but only basic skill in Oxygen. Venus has 2-star skill in both Power *and* Oxygen. So move Stig over from the Oxygen console to the Power console. Then select Venus and left-click on the Oxygen console to assign that as her Primary Job, bumping Nutrient Extractor down to secondary status.

> It's okay to shift Venus to the Oxygen desk. By now you should have several canisters of Base Nutrients stored in your warehouse tank, enough food to get by for several days.

It takes a while, but eventually Tami gets the base in pretty good shape. When the base litter is reduced to zero, you satisfy the first mission requirement. ***Objective completed.***

Add a Hygiene Pod

Of course, your colonists are getting ranker by the minute, too. To boost their Hygiene rating, they need to bathe. But where?

Click the Furniture button to see the new stuff you have available. Aha! For just 200 credits, you can pick up a snazzy Personal Hygiene Pod, which includes shower *and* toilet. Drop it in next to the Cleaning Post in the Medium Bio Dome. (It won't fit in the Small Bio Dome with all those beds in there.)

Check your people's Hygiene ratings and direct anyone with cleanliness problems to the shower. Remember that they'll bathe of their own accord, too.

3-13. Man, there's just nothing like a good session in the Personal Hygiene Pod!

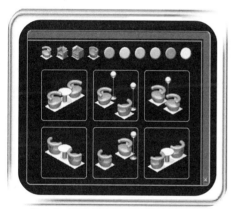

3-14. Install a Social Area customized to fit your personal social needs.

Build a Friendship

Now we can focus on getting things worked out between Stig and Tami. Here's a bit of advice: Small talk ain't gonna cut it here. They must become friends. So let's add a bit of furniture to make a deeper bonding experience possible.

Click Furniture and select the "Social Area"—a double-chair unit built to facilitate friendships. You get a Social Area selection window where you can customize the unit. Just select the style and color you want from the choices at the top of the window. Then click on the configuration you want and place the unit wherever you want it in the Medium Bio Dome.

The Social Area adds another option to social interactions between colonists: "Friendship." Just what we want!

3-15. Stig and Tami just need a good sit-down to air out their differences. The Social Area offers a new option to their Human Contact selection menu: "Friends." Go for it!

Select Tami, then click on Stig. (Or vice versa.)
From the three social interaction choices, select
Friendship. Tami and Stig will plop down in the
Social Area and talk through their differences.
If their relationship has sunken really low on the
Enemy scale previously, it may take a couple of
these Friendship sessions to get them to Friend
status.
Objective completed.

3-16. Success again!

MISSION: *GARDEN OF EDEN*

Background

"Iron deposits have been detected to the north of you. Investigate the newly opened zone and
locate the marker beacon to find the iron. Scans also report quantities of rapidly spreading vegetation in this area along with associated primitive alien activity. This must be cleared away before
extraction of the iron can begin."

Main Objectives

- Find the marker beacon.
- Eradicate the encroaching vegetation.
- Place one Space Bike Post.

New Operatives

Name: Dean Jefferson Brown

Mission Job: Weeding
Backup Job: Power or Oxygen

New Stuff Available

- ⊑⊏ Weeding Post
- ⊑⊏ Banking Console
- ⊑⊏ Space Bike Post
- ⊑⊏ Small Bio Dome
- ⊑⊏ Corridor
- ⊑⊏ Running Machine
- ⊑⊏ Stair Climber
- ⊑⊏ Rowing Machine

The Walkthrough

Say hello to new operative, Dean: friendly, intelligent, and an excellent MediPrep technician (although that skill is of no use right now). Dean's a bit obsessed with cleanliness–his Hygiene rating drops faster than the other colonists. So keep Dean showered, and keep things tidy around the base.

But wait: You can click the Pause button (top-right) and complete two mission objectives before the new guy even gets down the shuttle ramp.

Light the Way to the Marker

The iron deposits are northeast of the colony base, so that section of the Forbidden Zone is now open. Your job: Light the route to the marker. Our job: Make sure you do so efficiently, without wasting money.

Place the first Light as far north of the Solar Power Plant as possible. It illuminates a narrow canyon running north of some operational zone markers, glowing green now instead of red because that section of the Forbidden Zone is no longer off-limits. Place a second Light at the most northern edge of the illuminated area.

> **Lupulus**
> This weed is harmless enough, but it spreads rapidly and will soon clog up your base.

3-17. Light the north canyon that's overgrown with Lupulus and Podulus Toxicaria, then run Lights east to the marker beacon.

Note the Lupulus weeds sprouting everywhere. This is the "vegetation encroachment" you must halt. You may also find some red-flowered Podulus Toxicaria, home to Mutant Bees. This is bad stuff that must be eradicated. But we'll get to that task in a moment. First, let's find that beacon.

At an intersection of canyons, place another Light to the east (right) to find the marker beacon. Check out those lovely iron deposits by the beacon.
Objective completed.

Speed the Commute

A Space Bike speeds up transit across the planetary surface *considerably*. This makes the commute from your colony base to your exterior work sites (such as the Weeding Posts you'll soon place) much more efficient.

Select "Space Bike Post" from the Engineering menu, and place it as close to any colony airlock as possible. Now when an operative heads out to his Weeding Post, he spends a lot less time getting there. That means more time to charbroil Lupulus and Podulus with the old flamethrower. *Objective completed.*

3-18. Place a Space Bike Post next to an airlock in your Medium Bio Dome.

qwertyuiasl;zxcubam,.hjytfsz

We recommend placing the Space Bike next to the airlock leading from the Medium Bio Dome. This way, workers returning via Space Bike enter the base near the amenities (Mess Hall, Disco, Shower, etc.) you've placed inside that dome.

Weed Control (*Lupulus* and *Podulus*)

The Lupulus along the canyon looks innocent enough, but it's noxious stuff that spreads like wildfire; it will clog up your colony if you don't commit some serious herbicide right away.

Not only that, but Podulus Toxicaria may start growing, too. This plant spawns Mutant Bees the size of pumpkins; their vicious swarms can sting anything moving outside the base.

Fortunately, what you need for weed control is available now. Click the Industry button, select "Weeding Post," and place one just north of the green boundary lights at the mouth of the canyon. Place a second Weeding Post up the canyon at the intersection where it branches east toward the marker beacon.

3-19. Place a pair of Weeding Posts up the north canyon. Assign Dean to work at one until he clears that area, then assign him to the other.

Assign a Weeder

Go ahead, un-Pause now and let Dean enter the base. Only Stig and Dean have Weeding listed amongst their skills. Since Dean doesn't have a job yet, select him, then click on the Weeding Post to assign the task to him.

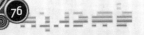

Room for Dean

While Dean toasts weeds, add a bed for him in the Small Bio Dome, which now has four beds and room for nothing else. Remember to assign Dean to his bed by selecting him and then clicking on the bed. (Be sure to note his personalized bedcover.)

Monitor your other workers' needs while the weeding proceeds. Keep your colonists happy and healthy! Between his shifts, give Dean a shower. Give Stig plenty of food between his work shifts at the Power desk; give Tami occasional Small Talk sessions with Venus. Keep Tami working from the Cleaning Post. If food starts to run low (though it shouldn't), trade Venus back and forth between the Oxygen console and Nutrient Extractor.

> Check Dean's skills; he's best qualified as a MediPrep technician. But since you don't have access to Medical Bays yet, Dean can't operate the Medical console in the Bridge. That comes in the next mission.

Add an Exercise Room

If you're feeling spendthrift, you can add a third Small Bio Dome connected by corridors to your Small and Medium Bio Domes. Consider adding one or two of the new exercise machines available in the Entertainment menu—Running Machine, Stairclimber, or Rowing Machine.

Both Dean and Venus find working out to be a particularly relaxing and invigorating form of entertainment (i.e., raising their Entertainment rating), and the other colonists will use the equipment regularly, too—except for Tami, of course.

Keep Weeding

Ridding the canyon and base area of weeds takes several work shifts for Dean. If you find Podulus Toxicaria plants somewhere along the canyon, immediately assign Dean to work at the Weeding Post nearest those noxious plants.

3-20. Both Dean and Venus love to work out, so build an exercise room in a separate Bio Dome.

> If weed growth seems to be getting out of hand, assign Stig to the second Weeding Post. Stig and Dean working together can eradicate the herbal menace quickly.

3-21. Another little victory.

If you're too late, and Mutant Bees spawn from the Podulus plants, just ignore them and keep working. The stings hurt Dean, but they aren't debilitating, and medical help is on its way in the next mission. When the last weed burns to a crisp, you win.
Objective completed.

MISSION: IRON IN THE VALLEY

Background

"You are cleared to begin iron extraction. Expand your warehouse area and stockpile all acquired iron there. Medi-bays are now available to help with Mutant Bee injuries."

Main Objectives

- Acquire 10 units of iron.
- Place new Warehouses—base total of three.

New Characters

Name: Candy Simpson

Mission Job: Cleaning
Backup Job: None (must be trained)

New Stuff Available

- Iron Extractor
- Warehouse
- Medical Bay
- Virtual Shop

The Walkthrough

Your "Win Conditions" are to mine iron and build Warehouses, but you can do a lot of intelligent base expansion with the tools now available. Pause the game as soon as Candy leaves the shuttle and is introduced to the colony.

Get Ready for Candy

First, get things ready for Candy's arrival. Since your bedroom is now full with four beds, build a new Small Bio Dome. Connect it with corridors to both the old bedroom and the Medium Bio Dome "activity center" where your Mess Hall and Personal Hygiene Pod are.

Put in a bed and assign it to Candy. And if you want to keep her, like, totally happy, install a Virtual Shop somewhere. Candy finds nothing quite as entertaining as scrolling through life's possibilities—especially if they're on sale.

3-22. Time to start another Bio Dome bedroom. Put Candy's bed here.

New colonists arrive in nearly every mission, so building a new Small Bio Dome now for Candy's bed is a good idea.

Add a Medi Bay

Either Dean or Stig may be suffering from lowered Health due to Mutant Bee stings. And Stig may be low on health from an earlier bad encounter with Tami. But now you have Medi Bays available, as well as an excellent Medi Prep technician in Dean.

Click the Human Resources button and select a Medi Bay, then place it in your larger Bio Dome. Assign Dean to the Medi Prep console in the Bridge. When the Medi Bay is prepped—you hear an announcement stating such—send Dean or Stig (or whoever is hurting most) to the Medi Bay to be healed.

3-23. A fully prepped Medi Bay restores full health to injured or sick colonists. With Mutant Bees about, it's wise to install one of these.

3-24. Drop an Iron Extractor next to the iron deposits by the marker beacon and assign Stig to work there.

Start Iron Mining

Now let's get down to business. Select the Iron Extractor from your Industry menu and place it next to the iron deposits near the marker beacon.

Select Stig and assign him the task of running the extractor; he's your best miner, with three stars of Mining skill. When he needs a break, you can spell him with Venus if she's free; she's the only other colonist with Mining skill.

Job Shifts

With Stig gone, move Tami back to the Power desk, then assign Candy to the Cleaning Post. After Dean preps the Medi Bay, send him back out to the Weeding Post to fight the Toxicaria infestation as it encroaches on the base. You don't want a bunch of Mutant Bees slamming into your facilities, lights, and equipment.

Don't ignore the rest of the colony as Stig mines the iron deposits. Keep things clean, keep folks talking and eating and exercising, and for gosh sake, don't forget the Power and Oxygen consoles.

Bike, Don't Walk!

Avoid building long Corridors between your Bio Dome areas. Walking is slow, while Space Bikes are speedy fast. So install multiple Airlock exits in each Bio Dome, then put Space Bike Posts next to the Airlocks that get the heaviest traffic to reduce overall travel time.

Add Two More Warehouses

As you stockpile iron (and later, other materials) from your extraction activities, you need someplace to store it. You have one warehouse area next to your Shuttle Pad—you've already stored liquid base nutrient there from your Nutrient Extractor. Let's add more warehouse space.

Just select "Warehouse" from your Engineering menu and place it adjacent to the other warehouse space. Repeat so you have three Warehouses. Note that adding each new Warehouse also adds another warehouse droid to your colony. You can never have too many warehouse droids, we always say.
Objective completed.

3-25. Add two more Warehouses for a total of three in your base to meet another mission objective.

qwertyuiasl;zxcvbnm,.hjytfsz

Keep an eye on the canyon area! Weeds and bees will pop up occasionally. Send someone with Weeding skill out to the Weeding Post nearest to the problem.

Keep Stig mining away. When your warehouse droid delivers the tenth stack of iron ore, your mission is accomplished.
Objective completed.

3-26. Way to go, Stig! A major miner success...

MISSION: *BOB AND BOFFIN*

Background

"Use the library facilities to train up members of the team. To demonstrate our ability for the coming rush, Mr. Waterhouse has set us a modest target for Space Chicken production. In response to a request from Venus, some extra recreational facilities have been made available."

Main Objectives

- Train Candy to Basic skill level in Chicken Extraction.
- Train Nikolai to Basic skill level in Chicken Extraction.
- Acquire 60 units of processed Space Chicken.

New Characters

Name: Billy Bob Perkins
Mission Job: Chicken Extraction
Backup Jobs: None in this mission!

Name: Nikolai Vokov
Mission Job: Power (for now, anyway)
Backup Job: Chicken Extraction

New Stuff Available

- Forcefield Post
- Chicken Farmer Unit
- Oxygen Plant
- Medium Bio Dome
- Library

- Bar
- Restaurant
- Jacuzzi
- Sauna
- Detention Facility

3-27. Your time is limited in this mission. Get right to work!

The Walkthrough

This is your first mission with a time limit—the "Time Until Defeat" timer at the top of the screen. You also have a Lose Condition. If just one colonist dies, mission over, you lose. So you should get right to work on your two objectives, which are both long-term projects. Hit Pause and start constructing immediately.

Meet Your New Operatives

Billy Bob is—well, he's not a bright guy. But he's one heck of a chicken farmer. Four stars good, in fact. And he has other basic skills, all physically oriented: Weeding, Maintenance, Cleaning, and Nutrient Extraction. But this mission is all about chicken farming, and Bob's your guy.

Nikolai is Billy Bob's polar opposite. He has double-star skill in such advanced topics as Electronics, Bio Research, and Pharmaceuticals, and single-star skill in Cybernetics and Scavenging—none of which is helpful in this mission. Fortunately, he also has single-star proficiency in Power and Oxygen, which does help for now. Nikolai is also a very quick study, which serves you well with your current needs.

Start Chicken Farming *Immediately*

Don't wait on this! Pluck a "Chicken Farmer Unit" from your Industry menu and plop it down west of your colony base. (You may need to place a Light near the western boundary markers first.) Make sure you have a few Air Locks at regular intervals in your Bio Dome walls, including one as close as possible to the chicken farm's control cab. You might also want to add an extra Space Bike Post.

3-28. Immediately drop in a Chicken Farmer Unit west of the base and get Billy Bob right to work. Don't assign him a secondary job—keep him totally focused on chicken farming.

Then immediately put your new colonist, Billy Bob, to work in the control cab. Don't assign him a secondary job!

Get the point here? Your key to mission success: Get your Chicken Extraction workers to and from the job *fast*, so your chicken farm has as little downtime as possible. To win, you must stockpile 60 units of Processed Space Chicken before the timer expires. That's a *lot* of units.

With a whopping 4 stars of skill in Chicken Extraction, Billy Bob is your main man in Mission 5. He should do almost all of the work in the Chicken Farming Unit. But when Billy Bob needs a break, don't let your farm suffer any downtime. Once you get Nikolai trained in Chicken Extraction, keep him ready to spell Billy Bob at the farm.

Build a Library

Billy Bob is already well qualified in the fine art of Chicken Extraction, but none of your other colonists has the requisite skill. Your other main mission objectives are to train both Nikolai and Candy to a basic skill level in Chicken Extraction. You need a Library for this.

By now, however, your Bio Domes are packed with furniture and other units. So a little intelligent expansion is in order. Place a new Medium Bio Dome just southeast of your first Medium Bio Dome. Install an Air Lock to ensure an easy route to the chicken farm.

Now select "Library" from your Human Resources menu and put one in your new Medium Bio Dome.

 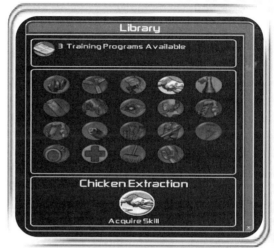

3-29. Drop in a new Medium Bio Dome and place a Library to train Nikolai and Candy in Chicken Extraction.

Train Two More Farmers

Nikolai is a much faster learner than Candy, so let's train him first so Billy Bob has backup as soon as possible. Select Nikolai and click on the Library to get the Library training menu. Click on "Chicken Extraction" and then click the Assign button at the bottom of the menu. Nikolai heads for the Library to bone up on space poultry.

Note that a "study counter" over Nikolai's head (see 3-29) starts counting down from 1,000. When the counter reaches zero, Nikolai's training is complete.

A person studying in the Library may leave in the middle of their training session to take care of some urgent need. When he/she returns, the study counter resumes right where it left off.

When Nikolai is fully trained in Chicken Extraction, assign that as his primary job. Now select Candy (a much slower learner) and give her the same instruction in the Library. Do it right away—Candy takes a *long* time to learn the skill. When she eventually finishes her training, you've met the first mission requirement.
Objective completed.

> *Remember: you have a Lose Condition, too. If just one colonist dies, you fail the mission. So keep an eye on everyone's Health need bar, particularly the colonists you send to work outside the base.*

Upgrade Your Base

Add beds for Billy Bob and Nikolai—don't forget to assign them both. Then start upgrading your base.

As you stockpile Processed Space Chicken, remember that your colonists have worked hard (mostly) and deserve some upgrades. This mission makes a lot of neat new stuff available for purchase. Plus, if you're following this walkthrough, you have a big, new Medium Bio Dome with lots of extra space.

First, upgrade your infrastructure. By now you should have some surplus iron stockpiled from Stig's mining work. Sell 10 units of iron to build up your bank account. Then add a couple of Solar Power Plants to give you more juice for the new facilities and machinery you're adding.

> *The Restaurant is now available in your Food and Drink menu, but we suggest you wait until the next mission to add one. Restaurant fare is based on succulent Space Chicken, so it draws from your processed stock. In this mission, you want to stockpile every bit of your Processed Space Chicken to reach the 60-unit target before the "Time Until Defeat" timer expires.*

Now reward your workers a bit with some new amenities. First, focus on fun. A Jacuzzi (now available on the Recreation menu) is a good way to satisfy the Entertainment needs of most colonists, but at half the cost and roughly the same Entertainment value for your current crew, you can get a Sauna instead.

3-30. Add a couple of new Solar Power Plants, then reward your colonists with a Sauna and Bar.

> *Stig loves the Sauna much more than he does the Jacuzzi, while the other colonists have roughly equal feelings towards both. So if money is tight and you can only choose one, take the Sauna. (It's cheaper, anyway.)*

We also like the Bar in the Food and Drink menu. Tami and Stig both *love* this facility. And it's relatively inexpensive—only 250 credits—plus Venus and Candy get some Entertainment satisfaction from it, too.

Invest in Protection

You have your first Military Systems unit available: the Force Field Post. When you place more than one of these posts, an electrical force field barrier flows between them. It doesn't harm your colonists, but it's strong enough to zap bugs—like, for example, those annoying Mutant Bees buzzing the canyons.

Run a zigzagging string of Force Field Posts from the base up the north canyon. If you can afford it, plant at least four posts. This should help keep your Mutant Bee problem under control.

If you're not bankrupt yet, you can add a second Social Area and Cash Machine in your new Bio Dome. Then, if you have cash left, add another Space Bike Post outside and another piece of workout equipment to your exercise room.

3-31. The Force Field Post is a good investment, but you need more than one to create the protective field. Run a few posts up your north canyon to zap bees.

3-32. Like, you win! And Candy totally learned something!

Beat the Clock

Don't let your colony-upgrade activities distract you from keeping your Chicken Farm Unit running without pause. Your "Time Until Defeat" is 18 days, with each day announced as the clock counts down. This means you should try to process about 4 units per day to stay on track.

Also, don't neglect the basic needs of your colonists, or let the basic functions (Power and Oxygen) of the base deteriorate. Keep people working, keep them happy, and keep extracting those Space Chickens.
Objective completed.

MISSION: *SPACE CHICKENS!*

Background

"You are required to achieve the positive credit rating outlined below. To help achieve this, a Silicon rich zone has been opened to you and extraction facilities are now available."

Main Objective

Achieve a credit balance of 20,000.

New Characters

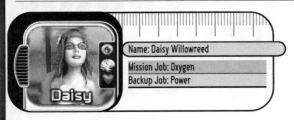

Name: Daisy Willowreed

Mission Job: Oxygen
Backup Job: Power

New Stuff Available

- Silicon Extractor
- Counseling Robot
- Engineering Repair Facility
- Zero Gravity Playroom

The Walkthrough

This mission introduces a new industry, Silicon Extraction. However, the overall mission goal is to make money, and right now the price of space chicken is sky-high. So your real objective in mining Silicon is to clear space for another Chicken Farming Unit as soon as possible.

> You can always sell off old stuff if you want to upgrade to new stuff—or if you just want the extra cash. Here's how:
>
> Click on the dollar sign icon just above the mini-map in the lower-left. Your cursor changes to a dollar sign. If you move this dollar-sign cursor over something you've previously purchased, you see the object's depreciated worth. Click on the object if you want to sell it off for that depreciated amount.

Add a Bed for Daisy

First, put another bed in your bedroom Bio Dome and assign it to your new colonist, Daisy. Hey, it's just common courtesy.

Daisy is a very organic. She's not unintelligent, and she brings a number of skills to your colony, including two stars in Bio Research—unfortunately, this skill isn't needed yet. Daisy is not what you'd call a go-getter. She takes a lot of naps. Indeed, her Sleep needs are prodigious, legendary.

Assign her to work the Oxygen console and move Tami back to her best job, Cleaning.

Sell Off What You Can

By now you've most likely mined all the iron deposits available on Catherwood. So sell off your Iron Extractor by clicking the Sell Base Structures button, then clicking the dollar-sign cursor on the rig.

Next, sell off your inventories. Click the Go to Bridge button and open the Trade Controls window. Sell off *all* your stockpiled Iron and Processed Space Chicken. Remember, your goal here is to attain a big credit balance.

3-33. Regularly sell off stockpiles in your Trade Controls window to build the credits you need for mission success.

3-34. Place a Silicon Extractor near the silicon deposits just west of your base. Your first goal: Mine them out to make room for another chicken farm.

Clear Silicon for More Chicken Farming

As the mission opens, a new section of the Forbidden Zone opens to the west. Select Pause and place a few of Lights running west from your colony. This illuminates numerous Silicon deposits between lava fields and a bubbling, black-water lake.

Again, your most lucrative industry is chicken farming. But you can't place any new farms here because of the Silicon deposits. The least-cluttered area is just west of your base—east of the lava and south of the lake—where only a few Silicon Crystals jut from the ground. Let's mine this area first.

Select the "Silicon Extractor" from the Industry menu and place it next to the Silicon deposits near the west end of your base. (You can't place the rig atop Silicon deposits or lava.) Do not un-Pause the game yet! Lava fields are dangerous on Catherwood. So let's make two investments to protect your Silicon Extraction operation before we actually install the actual mining facility.

Invest in Protection

Yes, lava hurts. But the lava itself isn't the problem here—you can find plenty of solid earth for your Silicon Extractor, and your commuting miners can skim over molten patches easy enough on a Space Bike. The problem is the pestilence known as the Lava Beetle.

You should have at least two Space Bike Posts by now. Add one or two more as you add exterior work sites, such as Silicon Extraction units. Avoid forcing your workers to commute on foot over lava and through swarms of Mutant Bees and Lava Beetles!

This toxic bug emerges from Catherwood's lava pits and wreaks havoc on your equipment and facilities with its blistering bite. How do you deal with such a beast? You fight fire with fire.

3-35. *Deploy a grid of Force Field Posts to fend off the Lava Beetle menace to the west.*

Click on Military Systems and select the Force Field Post. Again, when you place more than one of these units, they generate a defensive electrical barrier that damages alien bugs (like Lava Beetles) that try to pass through it. Install a grid of four or five Force Field Posts between the lava fields and the area where you plan to install your Silicon Extraction unit.

Consider adding two extra Forcefield Posts just west of the colony—one at either end of the row of green boundary lights—as protection for your base facilities against wandering Lava Beetles.

The force field doesn't kill Lava Beetles immediately, but it damages them every time they crawl through the electrical current. Most of the meandering bugs eventually crawl through enough times to get exterminated.

While this is happening, add one more bit of protection for the mining equipment you'll place shortly.

Invest in Repair

Lava Beetles and Mutant Bee swarms can damage external facilities. If you want to keep your costly industrial units, then you should start repairing damage on a regular basis.

First, you need an Engineering Repair Facility. Select one from the Engineering menu and place it next to one of the Airlocks by the Bridge.

Next, you need a worker (or two, preferably) with Repair skill. Only Venus and Stig have this skill right now. Stig is too valuable a miner to use anywhere else. So order Venus to man the Engineering Repair Facility.

Move Your Silicon Extractor

Your mining operation clears out the Silicon deposits just west of the base in short order. Of course, now the mining rig itself is in the way. Use the Sell Base Structures cursor to sell off the Silicon Extractor.

3-36. Add an Engineering Repair Facility to keep your machinery running smooth.

3-37. Move your Silicon Extractor to this Silicon-rich area further west to make room for another chicken farm.

Place a couple more Lights west of the farm to find tons of Silicon, everywhere. Find a clear spot to place a new Silicon Extractor, surround the area (including the Lights) with Force Field Posts, and order Stig to start working that rig.

Build a Second Chicken Farm

Place a Chicken Farming Unit on the newly cleared spot and assign Candy to work there. Now you have the basis of a flourishing economy with good income potential.

More Colony Upgrades

You have more people and more facilities. This creates new stress on your colony's society and infrastructure. Do the following:

- Boost your power! Add three or four new Solar Power Plants to your energy grid. Keep Nikolai busy as your primary Power console worker.

- Enhance your colony's dining capability by adding a new Restaurant. Mess Hall food comes from base nutrient, but Restaurant fare is based on tasty Processed Space Chicken—and you've got plenty of that now.

- Stig will be in heaven if you pop for a Zero-Gravity Playroom. It's just the kind of thrill-seeking fun he's drawn to try.

Sell Your Goods

Whenever your warehouse area is full, click the "Go to Bridge" button, select the Trade controls panel, then click on the Silicon and Processed Space Chicken buttons and sell whatever goods you've accumulated. When you finally hit the 20,000-credit mark, you win!
Objective completed.

3-38. Congratulations! You've made Mr. Waterhouse even richer and more ruthless than he was before.

MISSION: *HEAT!*

Background

"The evac from Catherwood is being planned. Mr. Waterhouse has already taken profits from our account and sold off a number of our facilities, including all the solar power plants. The discovery of the lava field means we are now required to utilize lava power as the preferred energy source. The new expanded team is to be rested and bonded into a cohesive unit in readiness for special duties on a new, unnamed planet.

"Small lasers are available to deal with the lava dwelling life-forms. The small furry rodents that arrived recently on a trade ship seem to be harmless and, as such, are not programmed into the military targeting computers. With local nutrient bearing vegetation gone and a reluctance to provide any more credits on this planet, you must use the Bio Labs to provide for your food needs."

Main Objectives

- Achieve an overall base Happiness rating of 70 percent.
- Stockpile 10 units of Argon Gas.
- Dean and Candy must become "Special Friends."

New Characters

Name: Capt. Charles Wilmington
Mission Job: Weeding
Backup Job: Space Gas

Charles

Name: Vasilios Cosmos
Mission Job: Repair
Backup Job: Space Gas

Vasilios

New Stuff Available

- Lava Powerplant
- Automatic Laser
- Bio Laboratory
- Argon Gas Rig
- Virtuality Chair
- Luxury Bar

The Walkthrough

This is a fun, but tough mission—perhaps the first *really* challenging mission in the campaign. Two of your mission objectives are hitting numbers: an Average Base Happiness rating of 70 percent, and an Argon Gas canister stockpile of 10 units. The third objective is to arrange for Dean and Candy to become "Special Friends"—that is, to fall in love.

Here's one complication: A mysterious disease afflicts your colonists this mission, triggering an ongoing medical emergency. Naturally, bad health lowers overall Happiness. Plus your colonists start the mission with all seven Need bars at 50 percent. So until you get the epidemic under control, your Base Happiness target of 70 percent will be very hard to achieve.

3-39. What's causing the mysterious disease afflicting all of your Catherwood colonists?

3-40. Automatic Lasers are a nice military systems upgrade, but they use Argon Gas. Thus your gas stockpile objective takes longer to achieve.

Why the Numbers Fluctuate

Automatic Lasers, available this mission, need Argon Gas to operate. Freshly collected Argon Gas canisters go directly from your Argon Gas Rig to any empty Automatic Lasers first, then into your warehouse. If an Automatic Laser runs out of gas and no canisters are available from the Argon Gas Rig, the laser turret gets refilled from the warehouse stockpile.

So you may have stockpiled 10 Argon Gas units, satisfying the mission objective... or so it seems. But if a sudden Lava Beetle attack depletes an Automatic Laser's gas supply and you have no gas canisters coming forth from the Argon Gas Rig, a warehouse droid automatically hauls an Argon Gas canister from your warehouse stockpile to the laser—and suddenly, you have only 9 units in stockpile! The mission objective icon for "Stockpile Argon Gas," which previously disappeared, now reappears at the top of the screen.

Average Base Happiness fluctuates, of course, precisely because it is an average. As various colonists get happy or depressed, the average goes up and down. The good news is that once you achieve the Happiness-based mission objective, it *stays* "achieved" even if its numbers drop back down under the target threshold as you pursue other mission objectives. In other words, once you hit 70 percent Average Base Happiness, that mission objective icon disappears for good, even if the Happiness average dips back below 70 while you try to acquire the 10 units of Argon Gas.

Focus on Happiness, Not Income

You start with about 10,000 credits, so money isn't much of a concern. In this mission, generating income is far less important than in previous missions. Your general task: Assign activities that fulfill your people's needs and thus raise their Happiness levels.

For example: Chances are good you've got enough Processed Space Chicken in your warehouse to keep your Restaurant supplied for a long time. If so, Billy Bob should spend less time chicken farming and more time eating and sleeping and having fun and keeping healthy. In general, don't hesitate to pull people off the job to bump up their Need bars, *especially* if the mysterious disease has their Health rating down in the red.

Another example: Consider assigning both Candy and Tami to do nothing but work the Cleaning Posts; a spotless base raises everyone's sense of well being (especially Dean's).

qwertyuiesl;zxcvbnm,.hjytfsa

Dean must be free to work only at the Medical console, keeping Medi Bays prepped and ready.

Meet Charles

Two new operatives arrive via personnel shuttle. Put in a new Bio Dome bedroom and assign beds for both new operatives. Captain Charles Wilmington is ex-officer-corps, and quite an expert with the Manual Lasers (2-star skill), which would be great if you had Manual Lasers. But you don't, yet. We recommend you immediately assign him to the Weeding Post in the north canyon, keeping the Podulus under control. This frees up Dean to focus entirely on keeping the Medi Bays prepped—the most critical operative task this mission.

Meet Vasilios

The other fellow is very strange. His Psychiatrist's Report calls Vasilios "highly delusional" and notes his unsettling eagerness (some call it obsession) to "study the stars." Absolutely nothing entertains Vasilios except for a stargazing session in an Observatory. But you can't get an Observatory yet. So Vasilios' Entertainment need slowly and inevitably deteriorates throughout the mission. Fortunately, it drops about four times slower than normal.

Place the Power Plants

You have no more Solar Power Plants, but Catherwood pulses with volcanic power. Find the three volcanic vents in the lava field west of the colony, then place a Lava Power Plant (from your Engineering menu) on the each vent.

3-41. Find the three volcanic vents in the lava field west of the base. Place a Lava Power Plant over each one, then add three Automatic Laser turrets on the lava field perimeter to protect the facilities from Lava Beetles.

qwertyuiesl;zxcvbnm,.hjytfsa

This is Lava Beetle territory, so put at least three Automatic Lasers (from your Military Systems menu) on the edges of the lava field near the power plants. They can't fire without Argon Gas, but we're about to fire up our gas rig.

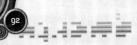

Fire Up the Gas Rig(s)

Select the Argon Gas Rig from your Industry menu and place it atop the gas bubbles emanating from the black crater lake northeast of the lava field. Send Venus and her two stars of Space Gas skill to work the rig.

If you want to speed up your laser activation, go ahead and put a second rig on the water. The sooner you get your Automatic Lasers deployed and loaded with Argon Gas canisters, the sooner you can stop worrying about pest infestations. Send Charles to work this second rig.

3-42. Put at least one Argon Gas Rig on the black water lake—two, if you can afford it.

Deploy Your Lasers!

Again, Automatic Lasers use up Argon Gas canisters, which you're also trying to stockpile in your warehouse. So place only as many Lasers as necessary. Keep in mind that your Automatic Lasers have excellent range, so you can get by with as few as five or six and still cover all the hotspots around the base. The next two sections suggest where to place your laser turrets.

Cover the Lava Fields

You must protect your Argon Gas Rig and Lava Power Plants. Place one laser near the Gas Rig and the second one halfway between the rig and your two Power Plants. Place a third laser directly south of the Power Plants, near the rocks. For insurance, place a fourth gun north of the Power Plants.

These four turrets should cover all of the Lava Beetle approach routes.

Double Up in Bee Alley

Now let's eliminate (finally!) the painful Mutant Bee menace that's been plaguing your poor Weeding Post workers in the canyon north of the base. Place *at least two* turrets just up the canyon. These lasers will remain very busy blasting swarms of Mutant Bees.

Be sure you still have a Weeding Post here, too, and keep a dedicated Weeding specialist assigned there. (Charles is a good candidate, unless he's working the second gas rig. If so, use Billy Bob for Weeding and leave the chicken farming to Candy.) His job is to torch the Podulus Toxicaria, keeping the bee swarms to a minimum.

Fill Your Gas Quota

With only six Automatic Lasers to refill, you should be able to stockpile Argon Gas canisters with relative ease now. When you stockpile about 15 units in your warehouse, you've got enough to keep you above the mission objective quota while you focus on the Base Happiness rating. *Objective completed.*

Meet the Health Emergency

3-43. Keep Dean free to do what he does best—prep Medi Bays.

But something odd is happening. If you've done even cursory Need scans of your 10 base operatives, you've noticed an alarming decline in basic health. Some sort of disease is hitting everyone hard, and one lousy Medi Bay won't cut it.

First of all, pull all miners and gas rig operators inside the base (you still need Weeding) and focus your attention on immediate Needs-gratification. Keep Nikolai on the Power console, Daisy on the Oxygen console, and Vasilios in the Engineering Repair Facility. Free Dean to focus solely on prepping Medi Bays to combat the mysterious illness affecting everyone.

Install at least one more Medi Bay, though a total of three is best. Keep cycling through your colonists, sending the sickest (lowest Health ratings) to prepped Medi Bays. If no Medi Bays are ready, keep your sick folks near the bays, topping off their other needs (eating, showering, checking the banking machine, whatever) until the next Medi Bay is prepped.

Add a Human Resources Center

With everything in place, oversee the individual needs of your colonists and respond to emergency situations (destroyed equipment, power shortages, Tami's rancid insults, etc.). If you have the credits, consider expanding your base a bit more by adding another Bio Dome and designating it your "Human Resources Center." Drop in a couple of items from your Human Resources menu—the Detention Facility and the Counseling Robot.

If you play smart, you probably won't need the Detention Facility in this mission. (Things haven't gotten totally crazy yet.) But the Counseling Robot is a perfect solution for Tami's incessant need for gab sessions. When your other colonists are busy but Tami is in a funk—that is, her Human Contact rating is low, as it often is—send her to the Counseling Robot. It's a slower fix than Small Talk, but it keeps her from tying up the valuable work time of your other colonists.

Other Happiness Tips

Here are a few quick tips for boosting the Average Base Happiness and, in general, enhancing the efficiency of the base:

3-44. Stig gains massive satisfaction from a sweaty session in the Sauna.

- Install plenty of Speeder Bike Posts. Put them near Airlocks to save a bit of flight time.
- Add another Social Area in a high traffic area and use it regularly to boost relationships into the Friendship range. The more friends you have in your base, the easier it is to raise Human Contact ratings in the long run with simple Small Talk encounters.

- If you've harvested up all the local Hydromorphus for food, you can build a Bio Research Lab and assign Daisy (with 2-star skill in Bio Research) to work there. Click on the lab and set the seeding choice to "GM Bamboo." The lab droid will plant bamboo shoots, which can then be harvested by your Nutrient Extractor and processed into food.

- Send Tami regularly to the Bar for her biggest Entertainment boost. And remember, she *hates* exercise.

- Candy really, really loves the Virtual Shop.

- Stig and Charles prefer the Sauna. Stig really digs the new Virtuality Chair, too, but the Sauna always comes first for him.

- Venus and Dean enjoy workouts on the exercise equipment, but Dean really dislikes drinking at the Bar.

- Billy Bob's favorite Entertainment facilities (available now, anyway) are the Zero Gravity Playroom and Virtuality Chair.

- Nikolai loves learning in the Library, but (along with Charles) deeply despises shopping.

- Daisy enjoys dancing and plants, but dislikes the thrill simulators.

If you keep all these things in mind, your Average Base Happiness will hit 70 percent in no time. ***Objective completed.***

MISSION: *EVACUATION*

Background

"No evac until all the Iridium has been collected. Advanced pharmaceuticals can now be purchased to combat the disease, but these are highly expensive and some colonist deaths are to be expected. Vasilios' request for an observatory has been granted."

Main Objectives

- Store 10 units of Iridium Crystals in your warehouse.
- Lose Condition: 3 colonists die.

New Characters

You gain no new colonists in this mission. You may, however, lose some.

New Stuff Available

- Electronics Fabricator
- Industrial Robotics Factory
- Scavenger Bunker
- Observatory

The Walkthrough

This mission seems simple on the surface—find some Iridium, mine a few units, done deal. But, of course, it turns out to be more complicated than that. A couple of unforeseen circumstances give you the opportunity to adjust on the fly. You can also experiment with two slick new industries, Electronics Fabrication and Industrial Robotics, although you can complete this mission without gearing up either one.

Find the Iridium Crystals

Here's the easy part. Just scroll the map to the lava field southeast of the base. It's already partially lit by glowing Photocyn mushrooms, so just place one Light on the eastern bank of the lava field. There it is—Iridium!

But as Venus points out, the Iridium Crystal patch is on the far (east) side of the lava field. You can't place your Scavenger Bunker on that side because rocks and the crystals themselves block placement. Plus there's no safe route across the lava field. So you have to put the bunker west of the lava.

But wait: Don't place the facility yet! Read the next section first.

3-45. Photocyn mushrooms provide natural illumination to some of the cavern areas, including the lava field next to the Iridium Crystal patch.

Lasers First, Bunker Second

You'll have to put your Scavenger Bunker on the near (west) side of the lava, forcing your poor Scavenger Robot to hotfoot it across the lava bed each time it gathers up an Iridium Crystal load. And don't forget: lava fields are home to the destructive Lava Beetle.

So before you place the bunker, put down an Automatic Laser turret nearby to keep any wandering Lava Beetles at bay. After you place the laser, wait a few seconds until warehouse droids can arm it with Argon Gas canisters. This secures the area.

Now you can place the Scavenger Bunker on the west bank of the lava field. We also suggest adding a nearby Space Bike Post to help reduce commute time for the long haul from the base to the bunker.

3-46. Place an Automatic Laser and a Space Bike Post next to your Scavenger Bunker; then assign Nikolai to work the facility.

Now pull Nikolai off the Power desk and send him (with his 1-star Scavenging skill) to operate the Scavenger Bunker.

As for your other workers: Put Charles on Power to replace Nikolai, keep Vasilios at the Engineering Repair Facility (very important—see next section), move Billy Bob to Weeding, and let Candy do your chicken farming. Keep Venus working the Argon Gas Rig, but make Scavenging her secondary job. Keep Stig mining Silicon for now—although you'll need him elsewhere shortly.

Robot Repair

After the very first few sizzling trips across the molten lava, the Scavenger Robot will be badly damaged. But you should have at least one Engineering Repair Facility up and running by this mission. If you don't, immediately build one and assign Vasilios to work there. Its repair droid should spend a lot of time hovering over your Scavenger Robot, keeping it functioning.

3-47. Keep your Engineering Repair Facility manned so the repair droid can repair the repeated lava damage to your Scavenger Robot.

3-48. Place an Observatory next to the Repair Facility where Vasilios works. You want to keep him happy so he works long hours.

Add an Observatory

You can see how Vasilios (running your Engineering Repair Facility) becomes *very* important in this mission. You want to keep him happy and working hard. Fortunately, the serene fellow finally gets something that entertains him—an Observatory. Place one next to the Engineering Repair Facility where Vasilios works.

Emergency! Targeting Systems Malfunction!

At precisely 00:00 on Day 3, Mr. Waterhouse suddenly appears onscreen to report a slight "glitch" in the military targeting systems. Translated from corporate-speak, he's actually saying, "Your base is entirely defenseless." All of your Automatic Lasers shut down! This leaves your colony totally vulnerable to both Lava Beetles and Mutant Bee swarms.

Military systems will remain offline until 0:00 on Day 7. It's a dire situation, and chances are good that bugs will destroy a Lava Power Plant or two, plus a few other smaller structures like Lights, Force Field Posts, and Automatic Laser turrets. But you can do a couple of things to survive the shutdown.

Add a Second Repair Facility

Quickly! Drop in a second Engineering Repair Facility. Pull Stig away from Silicon mining and put him in the new rig. He has a 1-star Repair skill, so he's your main man as you try to weather the defense-less stretch.

With two repair droids at work instead of one, you can keep your Scavenger Robot repaired as it crisscrosses the lava to the Iridium patch, while at the same time repairing damage from Lava Beetle attacks on your Lava Power Plants in the lava field west of the base.

3-49. Once the lasers go offline, construct a second Engineering Repair Facility and put Stig to work there.

3-50. Process your Silicon stockpiles into advanced electronics products in your Electronics Fabricator.

Robot Replacement: Two New Industries

Even with two Repair Facilities at work, it is possible to lose your Scavenger Robot to lava damage. To replace it, you can erect an Industrial Robotics Factory that's capable of manufacturing replacement robots of all kinds. Manned by Venus, this facility can crank out a new Scavenger Robot in a very short time.

However, each Scavenger Robot requires raw materials—two units of Iron, and two units of Electronics, to be exact. You have plenty of iron stockpile from the earlier missions... unless, of course, you sold it all. Don't worry, you can purchase more iron via the Trade Controls. But it's much cheaper to provide your own, of course.

You can also purchase Electronics via trade, but these are very expensive, too. A better idea might be to build your own Electronics Fabricator. This industrial unit processes pure Silicon (and you should have *plenty* of that) into advanced Electronics. Nikolai has a 2-star skill in Electronics, so pull him out of the Scavenger Bunker for a while to whip up 5 or 10 units of Electronics for new Scavenger Robot.

All of this industrial maneuvering becomes moot if you just keep your initial Scavenger Robot repaired. Again, if you have two Engineering Repair Facilities constantly going, your first Scavenger Robot should be fine.

Cure Your Colonists

Here's a better way to spend your cash. If you have a few thousand extra credits, you can buy some valuable Pharmaceuticals that cure your folks of the disease plaguing the base. Just click the Go to Bridge button and select the Trade Controls. Click on Pharmaceuticals and then select the Buy button to purchase five units.

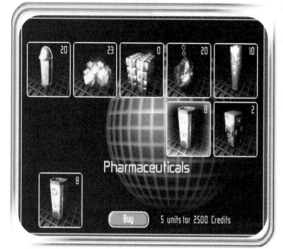 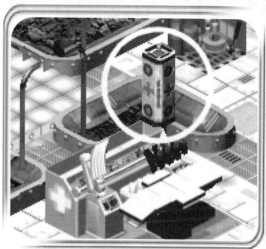

3-51. If you've got spare cash, buy a few units of Pharmaceuticals. With these drugs, Medi Bays can cure colonists of the disease.

Once the Pharmaceutical units are in your warehouse, droids deliver them to your Medi Bays. A Medi Bay loaded with drugs will cure a diseased colonist once and for all. This goes a long way toward ensuring mission success. Remember: If you lose just three colonists to the disease, you lose the mission.

Catherwood Success!

Once you get that tenth unit of Iridium stockpiled, your work on Catherwood is finished. Now you have a choice. You can select either the Civilian Path or the Military Path for the next set of missions. It doesn't matter which you choose—you can play both paths eventually.

3-52. Catherwood is history! Good job!

CHAPTER 4
CIVILIAN PATH:
THE PEACEFUL MISSIONS

Civilian Path
Peaceful Missions

Military Path
Fast Paced Missions

4-1. After you complete the Catherwood missions, you can choose the Civilian or Military Paths.

The Civilian Path focuses on industry and tourism, with a quirky alien twist thrown in at the end. Your first three missions along this path take place on the first planet of the Celensoan system, a world known simply as Celensoan A. For the final five missions, you shift locale to the second planet of the system, Celensoan 4b.

PLANET: CELENSOAN A
MISSION: *ANTIDOTE*

Background

"You are to stockpile nutrients and pharmaceuticals. Be advised, however, Stripper Insects have been detected on the planet. Speed is, therefore, of the essence as these creatures will strip the planet of all edible vegetation in a matter of weeks."

Main Objectives

- Acquire 15 units of Pharmaceuticals..
- Acquire 10 units of Base Nutrients

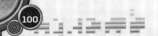

New Operatives

Name: Hoshi
Mission Job: Weeding
Backup Job: Power

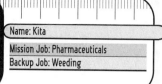

Name: Kita
Mission Job: Pharmaceuticals
Backup Job: Weeding

Name: Mr. Zhang
Mission Job: Cybernetics
Backup Job: None

New Stuff Available

- Pharmaceutical Extractor
- Large Bio Dome
- Relaxation Pod

The Walkthrough

Welcome to Celensoan A! Before the shuttle unloads your operatives, hit Pause and take a look around the area. Your new team arrives at a colony base with a Bridge and a complex of nearly empty Bio Domes. Inside, you have only your basic consoles, a Banking Machine, and a Cybernetics Lab.

You also start with some stockpiled resources in your nearby warehouses—a few Iridium Crystals, some Argon Gas and Base Nutrient canisters, and a *lot* of Electronics units.

4-2. Make a bedroom for Mr. Zhang adjacent to the Cybernetics Lab. Zhang needs a lot of sleep, so you want his bed near his workplace.

Prep the Base for Occupation

Place three beds in the empty Small Bio Dome. You should still have the game on Pause, so you'll assign the beds later, once the colonists actually arrive inside the base.

Place a Small Bio Dome adjacent to the dome with the Cybernetics Lab, connect the domes with a section of corridor, and then put the fourth bed in the new dome. This will be Mr. Zhang's bedroom. He needs a *lot* of naps and he's an excruciatingly slow walker, so it's best to put his bed as close as possible to the lab where he'll work.

Put in other basics: Mess Hall, Social Area, Personal Hygiene Pod, Cleaning Post, and one Medi Bay to start. Add a Running Machine for Venus, a Disco for Hoshi and Kita, and a Sauna for Mr. Zhang. (Put the Sauna in his bedroom for now. You can move it later.)

Outside, put in a couple of Space Bike Posts to speed trips out to the Weeding Posts and other outdoor jobs. Add two or three more Solar Power Plants to the power array, too.

Locate the Mounds

Outside, you start with a couple of Weeding Posts and only one Automatic Laser turret. But note the interesting vegetation, including a few patches of Cylincsus, the plant you must harvest for pharmaceuticals.

Unfortunately, ominous-looking Stripper Mounds sit next to several of the Cylincsus patches. If you move your cursor over a mound, you'll see these are home to the nutrient-eating Stripper Insects. That doesn't sound good.

Place a Light north of the Small Bio Dome with the lab to reveal still more Cylincsus and Stripper Mounds. Given what you know of Stripper Insects, you definitely want to eliminate the mounds and protect the plants.

Protect Your Resources!

Is the game still on Pause? Good. Now put another Weeding Post north of the base, in the midst of the Cylincsus. Place one Automatic Laser turret in each Cylincsus patch to guard against insect attack.

4-3. Place an Automatic Laser turret near every Cylincsus patch to protect the plants from Stripper Insects.

Stripper Insects are small, crawling bugs, so Force Field Posts can provide effective defense against them, too. Later, as your bank account builds, start placing posts in triangle or square patterns around Cylincsus patches.

Anti-Rodent Protection

Stripper Insects aren't the only infestation you must guard against. Every once in a while a gaggle of disease-carrying Rodents will make a rush for your base. Yes, they're cute and furry, but they carry the deadly plague that infected your crew back on Catherwood.

Keep adding Automatic Lasers around the base perimeter. In particular, focus on the area around the black water lake to the southwest. Four laser turrets in that area wouldn't be too many, trust us. The lake area seems to spawn regular insect and rodent swarms.

If some Rodents manage to infiltrate the base and infect colonists, send your people to the Medi Bay to raise their Health bar. Later, when you start manufacturing pharmaceuticals, your Medi Bays will cure the disease, too.

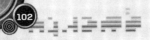

Build a Gas Rig

And do it right away. The sooner you get your laser turrets loaded and armed with Argon Gas canisters, the better. Place an Argon Gas Rig in the black water lake southwest of the base.

Assign Jobs

Okay, now you can un-Pause the game. Send colonists right to their first jobs as they enter the base from the shuttle. Send Venus to the Argon Gas Rig and get those gas canisters in production for the lasers. Send both Hoshi and Kita right out to two of the Weeding Posts and let them torch some Stripper Mounds.

When Mr. Zhang arrives, look at his skills—Cybernetics (4 stars) and Bio Research (2 stars). Impressive, but who's going to man the Power and Oxygen consoles while the girls get the Stripper Mounds toasted and lasers armed?

4-4. Androids step off the assembly table with high-level skills.

Build Androids

Answer: Androids. Send Mr. Zhang *directly* to the Cybernetics Lab. Again, Mr. Zhang is a 4-star superstar in Cybernetics. He assembles his androids quickly, and they are very helpful units.

Androids are "born" with an extremely impressive skill sets (see 4-4), so they should replace your colonists in various jobs as soon as Mr. Zhang cranks them out. Eventually, you should assign androids to the Medi Prep console, Weeding Posts, and Argon Gas Rig.

But for now, have the first android off the table work the Power desk. Once Power hits max on the gauge, put either Hoshi or Kita on Power and transfer the android to one of the Weeding Posts.

Install a Pharmaceutical Extractor

Now let's get to the mission objectives. First, place a Pharmaceutical Extractor (an indoor unit) in your Large Bio Dome. Assign an android to run it. If no android is available, use Kita or Hoshi until Mr. Zhang gets another fellow made.

The Extractor deploys its flying droid to hunt for "pharmaceutical-rich plant forms"—in this case, the Cylincsus. The droid brings back the plant extract, and then the Extractor converts it into medicine. Warehouse droids ferry the finished Pharmaceuticals to the warehouse stockpile.

4-5. A Pharmaceutical Extractor sends its droid to harvest the Cylincsus plants to make life-saving medicine.

The drug-making process is slow, so consider adding a second Pharmaceutical Extractor, manned by one of Mr. Zhang's androids.

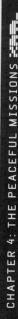

Add a Nutrient Extractor

Place a Nutrient Extractor facility next to any one of the groves of Hydromorphus trees around the base. Here's one where Venus outperforms any of the androids in terms of skill rating. So pull Venus from the Argon Gas Rig and send her to work the Nutrient Extractor. Have an android to take her place in the gas rig.

Monitor the Mound Growths

When you assign a colonist or android to a Weeding Post, she/it continues to work from that particular post, even if another Weeding Post is closer to where new noxious growths appear.

So when you get word of an attack on the base, hit Pause and locate the incursion. If it's a swarm of Stripper Insects, pinpoint their Stripper Mound and direct your Weeding worker (whether android or human) to the Weeding Post nearest the mound.

Again, if you don't do this, the worker automatically goes to her/its most recently assigned Weeding Post... which could be on the opposite side of the colony area, far away from the newly appeared Stripper Mound. Once dropped off by Space Bike, the Weeding worker then walks ever so slowly toward the new mound. If you don't reassign the worker to a post nearer to the mound, that can take a long time!

Wrap Up

If you've set up your lasers well and deployed your Weeding workers properly, you should easily and quickly produce the 10 units of Base Nutrients and 15 units of Pharmaceuticals you need to complete your mission objectives.

4-6. Victory! For now, anyway.

MISSION: CONTRACT RACE

Background

"Good news! Scans report there is Titanium here. Even better, the rights to exploit Celensoan's sister planet, 4b, are to be granted to the first company to hand over a consignment of the stuff to the local system governor as an inducement. As you might have noticed, Heron Mining is already operating on the planet, so let's get digging shall we?"

Main Objective

Acquire 50 units of Titanium.

New Operatives

Name: Slim
Mission Job: Oxygen
Backup Job: Weeding

New Stuff Available

- Titanium Extractor
- Iridium Power Plant
- Meditation Room

The Walkthrough

A race! It's your company of miscreants versus Heron Mining up in the northeast corner of the map. The foe has a head start, but you can eliminate that with some cutthroat business practices.

Place Lasers First and *Carefully*

Put two or three Automatic Lasers as far north as possible in the gaps between Titanium rows. (See 4-7 for the precise spot.) This exact placement is crucial. If you put lasers too far south or east, the Heron Mining laser turrets immediately destroy yours. But if you install your lasers in the right place, your turrets can reach *two* Heron Mining Titanium Extractors and destroy them without taking any return fire!

Keep Your Argon Rig Running

The Automatic Lasers you placed up north will expend a lot of Argon Gas as Heron Mining keeps trying to place facilities closer to the Titanium deposits. If your lasers run out of gas, chances are good that Heron will place a hostile turret in range and blast your inactive guns!

4-7. Immediately place Automatic Lasers at the top of the "row" in the deposits, as shown circled here. Then put your Titanium Extractors on the westernmost edge of the Titanium deposit field.

Keep your Argon Gas Rig working so you can keep your lasers topped off with gas canisters. Venus is your most skilled Space Gas specialist, so send her to work the gas rig for a while. You must build up a small stockpile of Argon Gas canisters to keep the edge up north!

Start Titanium Mining

Place two Titanium Extractors on the western side of the Titanium field (see 4-7) to keep out of range of enemy lasers. Just to be safe, put another Automatic Laser turret or two just east of the Extractors. (Not *too* far east, though, or they'll get blasted!)

Send Stig to work one rig. If you've got a stockpile of at least four Argon Gas canisters, send Venus to the other. Otherwise, wait until Mr. Zhang's first android hops off the Cybernetics Lab assembly table.

Build Android-Miners

Here's your ace in the hole. Androids come to life with 2-star Mining skill. Plus, they work tirelessly, without taking breaks, because they have no needs. As soon as the first android is available, send it immediately to whichever Titanium Extractor is not being run by Stig. (If Venus is working there, send her back to the Argon Gas Rig now.)

Train Minor Miners

Your androids are excellent miners, but here's a little tip: Slim, Hoshi, and Kita must train up to 2-stars in Mining skill as part of next mission's primary objectives. So let's get a head start. Place a Training Pod in your Large Bio Dome and train each teen up to a basic level in Mining. (It's expensive, so keep an eye on your credit balance.)

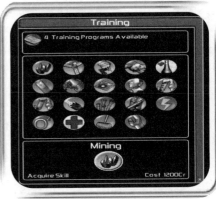

4-8. Put in a Training Pod and boost the Mining skill of your three teen colonists.

Let the Kids Dance

Hoshi, Kita, and Slim all love the Disco more than anything, and since Entertainment is a special need for the three kids, let them dance regularly.

While training one kid, order the other two to run the vital base functions, Power and Oxygen. Slim knows only Oxygen, but Kita and Hoshi have both skills, so you can keep both consoles active regardless of the pair working the desks.

Eventually, your laser attacks will take their toll on the Heron Mining output. Key: Keep those northern lasers loaded with Argon Gas! Their harassment of Heron lets you double your enemy's Titanium mining rate, especially with the skilled Stig and an android running your Extractors. If you followed our instructions, you win the contract race easily. Good job, team!

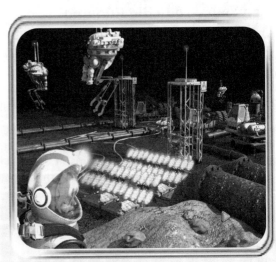

4-9. Black Water Industries 1, Heron Mining 0.

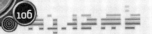

MISSION: PRESSURE COOKER

Background

"Evac from the planet is postponed until all alien pods have been recovered and sold back to the Federation. Little information is known about the target although signs of activity have been detected and a speedy collection is advisable. In preparation for the forthcoming assignment on 4b, the corporation has requested that several operatives be trained and receive their Silicon extraction badges."

Main Objective

- Stockpile 5 protoraptor pods.
- Train Hoshi, Kita, and Slim up to 2 stars in Mining.
- Lose Conditions: One colonist dies OR all protoraptor pods are destroyed before the required number collected.

New Operatives

Name: Greg Chesterton
Mission Job: Space Gas
Backup Job: Mining

Name: Babette Devereaux
Mission Job: Oxygen
Backup Job: None

Name: Bhoomi Sharma
Mission Job: Medi Prep
Backup Job: Cleaning

Name: Nailer McBride
Mission Job: Cleaning
Backup Job: Mining

New Stuff Available

- Titanium Extractor
- Iridium Power Plant
- Meditation Room

The Walkthrough

This may be the "Civilian Path," but you still get to blow up stuff. Protoraptor pods are scattered throughout the canyon basin to the east. But the crashed spaceship blocks passage into the pod area.

Build an Android

As the mission opens, send Mr. Zhang to his Cybernetics Lab to build an android. A dangerous task lies ahead, and you cannot lose even one colonist. (If a single colonist dies, you fail the mission.) The android can perform the dangerous task, sparing your colonists if something goes awry.

Destroy the Spaceship

Set four Automatic Lasers in the narrow canyon entrance just west of the crashed spaceship. That may seem like overkill, but you need them for more than just blasting the spaceship out of the way. A wave of vicious protoraptors will swarm the canyon entrance soon after the spaceship explodes.

Immediately order Venus to work the Argon Gas Rig. You need a bunch of gas canisters to fully load your quartet of laser turrets. Consider putting in a second gas rig and have the new guy, Greg, work there.

4-10. Place no fewer than four laser turrets in the canyon entrance, or else they'll be overwhelmed by the protoraptor rush after the spaceship is destroyed.

Remember to sell off your Titanium units via the Trade Controls button in the Bridge window.

Also, send Stig back to work at one of the Titanium Extractor rigs you placed up north last mission. You'll need the income from selling Titanium to pay for all the extra laser turrets early, plus you'll need big credit for the expensive training later in the mission.

Reinforce Your Base Defense

Make sure the eastern side of your base is well defended just in case the protoraptors manage to chew their way past your four canyon turrets. (They probably won't, but you never know.) Have two or three Automatic Lasers along the edge of the base near the canyon entrance.

Start Scavenging

After your four gun turrets decimate the first wave of protoraptors, put a Light in the canyon (near the canyon wall to leave room), and then place a Scavenger Bunker near your lasers. This is a precarious position, so staff the bunker with the newly built android.

Your Scavenger Robot starts collecting the pro-toraptor pods from the nests in the canyon. It can work only in well-lit areas, so if the robot stops collecting pods before reaching its quota of five, you probably need to place another Light further down the canyon.

Once your Scavenger Bunker processes the fifth pod, your mission objective is complete. To build your credit balance, you can now sell off the Scavenger Bunker if you want. Again, you need a good chunk of cash to train your teens up three levels of Mining skill.

If your android still has survival time left, put him on the Medi Prep console in the Bridge. You may need some ready Medi Bays in case the occasional Rodent infestation gets past your defenses and sickens any colonists.

4-11. Put in a Scavenger Bunker, but keep it within range of your four lasers for cover.

Keep Your New Staff Entertained

Once you reach your protoraptor pod quota of five, you can shift the primary focus back to your base—as long as you have a strong defensive perimeter of lasers and a few Force Field Posts, of course. Spend some time building up overall Happiness ratings in your colonists; satisfy basic Food, Sleep, and Hygiene needs, and then run people to their favorite activities. Get the base cleaned up, too—Nailer and Venus have that skill.

Your new recruits have their own favorite entertainment activities. As time goes by, put in anoth-er Large Bio Dome and add the following: Relaxation Pod for Bhoomi, Jacuzzi for Greg, Combat Arena for Nailer, and Piano for Babette.

4-12. Why do you suppose the Feds want protorap-tor pods?

Train Your Kids

Everybody happy? Excellent! Now you can finish up the mission objectives. Keep Stig and Greg mining the Titanium deposits in the northwest, then sell off the resulting stockpiles for some good income. You need this to train up Hoshi, Kita, and Slim to 2-stars apiece in the Mining skill.

The first training session, taking each teen up to a basic skill level in Mining, is 1200 credits apiece. The second session (adding one star of skill) is 2100 credits apiece; and the third session (going up to two stars of skill) is a stiff 3000 credits per kid. According to our crazy space calculator, that adds up to 18,900 credits. As Slim would say, that's some serious coin, jack.

But Titanium fetches a very good price on the market, so you should be able to afford all training sessions, and with income to spare. Keep your colonists healthy—again, if you lose even one oper-ative, you suffer mission failure. (Have Bhoomi keep those Medi Bays prepped!)

Once your teens are trained up, you win. Time to move on to another planet.

Celensoan 4B
Mission: Welcome to Our Home

Background

"Welcome to Celensoan 4b. The corporation has earmarked this planet as a possible site for its new flagship hotel. First we are to prove the viability of the planet as a tourist venue. You are to clear away the large Silicon deposits and use the resulting credits to found the tourist facility."

Main Objective

Attract 40 tourists within 60 days.

Operatives

The old gang's all here—Venus, Stig, Slim, Candy, Billy Bob, Hoshi, Kita, Mr. Zhang, Greg, Babette, Nailer, Bhoomi.

New Stuff Available

Single Room Hotel

Tourist Port

Slot Machine

Combat Arena

The Walkthrough

You start with a clean slate and 8000 credits in a brand new base on Silicon-rich Celensoan 4b. The colony has some basic amenities, but you should do some work before your colonists exit the shuttle.

Your ultimate goal is to attract 40 tourists in 60 days, but you have plenty of time to get things ready for the visitors. Once you place a Tourist Port, tourist shuttles start arriving once every four days, and each shuttle can unload multiple tourists. So technically, you can bring in 40 tourists in far fewer than 60 days.

That means you can take time to transform the bleak, Silicon-encrusted surface of Celensoan 4b into an attractive resort destination that fills up incoming tourist shuttles. No problem!

Buy Food First!

As Venus eventually points out, Celensoan 4b has no Hydromorphus trees as a food source. In the long term, you might want a Bio Research Lab to grow GM Bamboo for nutrient extraction. But in the short term, you need food *now*! Buy 10-15 units of Base Nutrients to get your Mess Halls and Bar loaded with food and drink to start.

Find Room for More Beds

You start with two bedroom Bio Domes, each with four beds already in place. But eventually, 12 workers will exit the shuttles. So you need another dome with four more beds. The problem is, Silicon deposits jut up everywhere, making it hard to find space. However, you can place a Small Bio Dome adjacent to the dome with Personal Hygiene Pod.

Prep the Base for Occupation

You start with some good stuff, including two Mess Halls, a couple of Social Areas, a Bar, and a Zero Gravity Playroom. But for gosh sake, put in a Disco! Your three kid-miners will need that dance floor between their work shifts.

4-13. Celensoan 4b is a silicon-encrusted wasteland. To build a resort, run multiple Silicon Extractors to open up development space.

Drop in a few more Airlocks so your miners have easy access to their rigs. Add at least three Space Bike Posts near high traffic Airlocks (those leading from the central Bio Dome), plus a few more Solar Power Plants and two more Warehouses.

Clear the Silicon Deposits!

It's a good thing you trained your teen colonists in Mining last mission. You need to clear out space in the Silicon deposits for hotels and Bio Domes full of tourist attractions. Now you have five good miners in Stig, Hoshi, Kita, Slim, and Greg.

> *Notice the four ominous monoliths southwest of the base, near the Forbidden Zone boundary line. These will have significance later, but they have no impact on the current mission.*

So before your workers step off their shuttle, place four Silicon Extractors in the deposits south and east of the base area. Spread them out evenly so the mining robots work more efficiently. Add a fifth Silicon Extractor to the northwest to clear out deposits for the extra warehouse space you'll need.

qwertyuiosl;zxcvbnm,.hjytfsz

> *If you want to direct a Silicon Robot to mine specific areas, just click directly on the robot (not the rig) and select "Set Mine Area" to get a placement cursor shaped like a green cone. Then click the cone on the area where you want the robot to focus its efforts.*

Now let your colonists arrive. The shuttles bring in four at a time. Assign Venus to the Power desk with Oxygen as her secondary job. Send Stig, Slim, Kita, Hoshi, and Greg out to the five Silicon Extractors.

Put Candy and Billy Bob on the Cleaning Post for now. Later, when you clear space, you can add a chicken farm (run by Billy Bob, of course) to keep your tourist-magnet Restaurants supplied with fine chicken products.

Add Warehouses

Drop in several more Warehouses to the northeast of your base. You don't need the warehouse space so much as you need the extra warehouse droids. By the end of the mission you'll have a lot of facilities that need refill from various warehouse stockpiles. Having a lot of warehouse droids keeps the refill process moving smoothly.

Sell Silicon to Build Credit

You don't need all the tons of Silicon you're mining. In fact, the silicon stockpiles do little for you right now, other than take up valuable warehouse space. So every couple of minutes, use the Trade Controls to sell off all your Silicon. Save up the credits until your Silicon Extractors finally clear a large area southeast of the colony base.

See page 65 in Chapter 2 for tips on constructing your tourist resort.

Start Your Resort

Again, technically, you can wait 15 or 20 days to place your Tourist Port and start the tourist influx. But that's leaving little room for error. By Day 10, you should have a large area cleared and plenty of banked credits from Silicon sales.

Sell back any Silicon Extractors sitting in the open area you've cleared. Then place a Tourist Port, a couple of Single Room Hotels, and a Large Bio Dome in adjacent positions. Connect this new complex with plenty of corridors, and pop a few Airlocks in place around the perimeters of these structures.

4-14. Put in a Tourist Port and a pair of Hotels to get started. Be sure tourists have access to the rest of your base.

4-15. Build a "Tourist Fun Center" for your visitors. Put in a nice variety of facilities.

Be sure everything is connected to your colony's existing activity area, so tourists have access to your Bar, Disco, and Zero Gravity Playroom, and Mess Halls in the early going.

Build a Tourist Fun Center

Now start filling up the new Large Bio Dome with stuff that tourists like. For precise stats, you can check the Tourists section at the very end of *Chapter 2, Character Profiles*. But here's a few tips for starters. Add the following items:

- *Restaurant.* Tourist Dads and especially Tourist Moms love it. Even tourist kids get a little enjoyment beyond just satisfying food needs.
- *Combat Arena.* Entertainment for the whole gosh darn family, believe it or not. (And Nailer will be eternally grateful.)
- *Jacuzzi.* Tourist females get a perfect 10 satisfaction from a soak in the tub, and the males like it, too. Of course, Greg absolutely adores this diversion.
- *Relaxation Pod.* Again, all family members (especially the females) get satisfaction from a rest in the pod.
- *Virtuality Chair.* You already have a Zero Gravity Playroom in your colonist area, and tourist kids will be attracted to that thrill attraction (especially boys). If you want to keep them more in their own area, put this chair in your Tourist Fun Center.
- *Cleaning Post.* Last, but not least! Resort cleanliness is a major factor in tourist satisfaction ratings. Keep Candy, Bhoomi, or Nailer at work here.

Keep Your Colonists Happy

Once you've got all of this stuff in place, your tourists take care of themselves. Spend the rest of your time keeping your colonists happy, so that nobody (like Stig) gets disgruntled and loses his mind or punches out a tourist.

Keep Your Equipment Repaired

The heavy tourist use will start to take its toll on mechanical equipment like the Jacuzzi and Zero Gravity Playroom. Check the status of your base facilities and equipment—just place your cursor over the equipment and look at its "health bar." Add a Maintenance Post when stuff starts to wear down. Assign Nailer or Billy Bob to this job.

If you stay on top of colonist needs and make sure your Tourist Fun Center is clean and working, you should get your 40 tourists with plenty of time to spare.

4-16. So you got your 40 chumps, er, tourists. Well done!

MISSION: *FAIRWAY*

Background

"The corporation is happy that the facility will work and now wishes you to go to Stage Two and increase the prestige of the resort. Our Bio Labs have now been kitted out to produce space grass, which will allow us to recreate a popular game from the last century. It was called Golf."

Main Objective

- Tourist must play five golf holes you've built.
- Greg and Babette must become "Special Friends."

Operatives

Dean and Vasilios join your entire crew from the last mission—Venus, Stig, Slim, Candy, Billy Bob, Hoshi, Kita, Mr. Zhang, Greg, Babette, Nailer, Bhoomi.

New Stuff Available

- Golf Tee
- Golf Hole
- Space Defense Shield
- Art Exhibit
- Double Room Hotel

The Walkthrough

This mission can be quick and lots of fun, if you've developed your resort properly and you get lucky (or rather, if Greg gets lucky). Mr. Zhang finally gets to do something useful, and you get to pair up the two most conceited colonists on your team. It's a love match made in heaven... or maybe Indianapolis, we're not sure.

In any case, think of it as two seeding projects. But first...

Protect the Base & Resort from Meteors

Deadly meteor showers plague Celensoan 4b in this mission. If you don't protect your colony with Space Defense Shields, the meteors destroy structures very quickly. So before you do anything else, place at least five Space Defense Shields at regular intervals around the perimeter of your colony resort complex. (Left-click on each shield as you place it to see the coverage range.) If you have any room between buildings, drop another one or two shields in the middle of the complex.

4-17. Start by placing Space Defense Shields for protection against killer meteor showers. Left-click on any shield to see the coverage range of all shields.

> *How much protection are you getting from a Space Defense Shield you've placed? To find out, just left-click on the unit. A green circle appears, indicating the exact range of the shield's coverage.*

It's a little expensive at 1000 credits a pop, but you can sell off more Silicon to bolster your bank balance. You probably have plenty of extra Processed Space Chicken in your stockpiles, too, if Billy Bob's been doing his usual job on your chicken farm. Sell enough stuff to get the Space Defense Shields. Your tourist industry will bring in credits soon, too.

Add a Bio Research Lab

To build a golf course, you need grass. And to grow grass, you need a Bio Research Lab. Place a lab adjacent to the bedroom Bio Dome where Mr. Zhang's bed is located. Put an Airlock in the dome so Zhang has easy passage from the lab to his bedroom. Remember: he needs a lot of naps. Then assign Mr. Zhang (with this 2-star skill in Bio Research) to work in the lab.

> *The in-game tips suggest you build several Bio Research Labs to green up the golf course faster. This isn't necessary to win quickly, but if you do build extra labs, Hoshi and Kita both have basic skill in Bio Research.*

Lay Out Your Golf Course

Ah, this if fun. You get to design your own space golf course. Open the Tourism menu and select the Golf Tee. Place the tee on the planet's surface, preferably right next to the Bio Research Lab to save seeding time. (We'll explain shortly.) When you click to place the first tee, it automatically numbers itself as "1."

Now move the cursor away from the tee. When it gets a short distance away, a Golf Hole appears (a flag and hole, actually). Notice that the flag is also automatically numbered "1". Move the first hole where you want it, and click to place it.

Select the Golf Tee from the Tourism menu again and place another tee and hole. Note that they automatically number themselves "2." Continue this process until you've laid out five golf holes. Be creative, but try to run holes side-by-side so your layout doesn't extend too far from the Bio Research Lab.

4-18. Layout your course near your Bio Research Lab. Run holes side-by-side to keep the course compact and reduce seeding time.

Seed the Course

Can your tourists play the course yet? Nope. You can't play golf without greens around each hole. (Holes you can't play are indicated with a slash icon over the flags.) You have to seed the green with genetically modified grass (GM Grass).

Click on the Bio Research Lab and make sure the "Currently Seeding" button is toggled to GM Grass. Then click on the "Set Plant Area" button to get a green, cone-shaped cursor. Click the green cone on the area you want to seed with grass—in this case, right next to the first golf hole.

> Seed only around the golf holes. You don't have to seed the tees or connect tee to hole with a "fairway."

This seeding process takes time for two reasons. First, the Bio Research Lab moves slowly. It often takes at least two "drops" by the seeding droid before the green is solid enough around each hole to allow play. Secondly, Mr. Zhang is an old guy with low endurance. He frequently leaves the lab because his Sleep Need bar drops so quickly.

However, if you placed the Bio Research Lab next to his bedroom Bio Dome as we suggested, you can minimize Mr. Zhang's lost work time. Also make sure a Sauna and Banking Machine are nearby, too, to best take care of Zhang's other major needs.

Place another Space Defense Shield right next to your golf course! You don't want a stray meteor to pulverize all your careful work.

While this seeding process plays out, you can spend time manipulating the romantic relationship between Greg and Babette. Just be sure to check back regularly; move the "Set Plant Area" for the lab seeding droid to the next golf hole after each hole is green and ready.

Eventually, all five holes are playable. But the mission objective isn't completed until a tourist actually plays all five holes.

The Greg and Babette Thing

You did this with Dean and Candy back on Catherwood, so you should be familiar with the process of stoking the hearth fires of love. Start with a "Friendship" talk in the Social Area to get them on friendly terms, then start the courtship by clicking the Romance button and proposing dates.

But wait—here's a big, *big* tip. If Babette does the asking, your chances of success are much greater than if Greg asks the questions. In fact, if she asks him for a Jacuzzi date, she has a 100 percent chance of success!

Here's a comparison that shows exactly how much greater your chances are by letting Babette be the aggressor:

4-19. Let Babette do the asking in her courtship with Greg. Her chances of success are much greater than vice versa.

IF GREG ASKS BABETTE

Greg's Question	Base Percent Chance Babette Says "Yes"
Let's go eat.	40
Want to get a drink?	60
Shall we dance?	50
Let's work out!	40
Come to the sauna?	50
Dip in the Jacuzzi?	50
Will you be mine? (3 Hearts)	40

IF BABETTE ASKS GREG

Babette's Question	Base Percent Chance Greg Says "Yes"
Let's go eat.	80
Want to get a drink?	80
Shall we dance?	80
Let's work out!	80
Come to the sauna?	80
Dip in the Jacuzzi?	100
Will you be mine? (3 Hearts)	60

Big difference, there. Man, do you see why strategy guides are so valuable?

In the end, Babette wins over Greg easily. If you've protected your base with Space Defense Shields and micromanaged the golf course seeding a bit, you should finish this mission pretty quickly.

4-20. Another mission accomplished!

MISSION: THE CELENSOAN RITZ

Background

"You are to improve and expand facilities at the base to create the galaxy's first 10-star hotel."

Main Objective

- Achieve a Tourism Rating of 10 stars.
- Achieve a credit balance of 100,000.

New Operative

That good 'ol gal, Tami La Belle, returns to your team for this mission. You also get a new operative.

Name: Barbara Leechworth

Mission Job: Power
Backup Job: Oxygen

Barbara

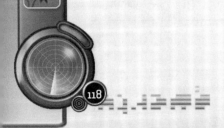

New Stuff Available

- Garden Dome
- Zoo Exhibit
- Viewing Platform
- Manual Laser
- Triple Room Hotel
- High Power Force Field
- Hover Mine Delivery System

The Walkthrough

Unlike the last mission, this one requires some time—hours, probably. You're building a massive super hotel and a huge credit account, so patience and attention to detail are required. You have lots of swell new stuff available to wow your tourists, so take advantage of that.

Expand Your Mining Operation

Keep your five silicon miners working. While much of your treasury buildup to 100,000 will come from tourists (1000 for each new tourist who arrives), your mining operation will finance a large part of the expansion. Silicon fetches a healthy 1000 credits for every 10-unit batch you sell… and if you've done any scouting (placing Lights leading away from the base), you know that Celensoan 4b has *vast* stores of Silicon deposits. So keep four or five Silicon Extractors busy.

Expand Your Resort

Some of the new Tourism menu items are exterior structures. Others go inside. Build another large Bio Dome and add some of the following items around your tourist area:

- **Viewing Platform.** Scores a perfect 10 in Entertainment value for all tourists, young and old. Very expensive, though, at 7500 credits.
- **Zoo Exhibit.** This also gets 10s across the board from all tourists. Affordable, too, at only 500 credits per exhibit. (Billy Bob loves the zoo, too.)

- **Piano.** All tourists enjoy music, especially the young girls. This is an excellent addition to your Tourist Fun Center. (It's also Babette's favorite entertainment.)
- **Garden Dome.** Another exterior structure enjoyed by all.

4-21. The Viewing Platform and Zoo Exhibits from your Tourism menu are two sure-fire hits that will delight all four tourist types—Mom, Dad, Boy, and Girl.

Spend Your Surplus!

You should reach the 100,000-credit mark long before you reach the 10-star Tourism Rating. In fact, you may just build up a huge credit surplus. You will lose most of it when the next mission starts, so don't waste it—spend it now! The next three tips suggest how to do that.

Train Up Your Operatives

Add a Training Pod somewhere in your colonist living area. The best bang for your buck over the long haul comes from boosting your operative skill levels. It's expensive, particularly as you train to the higher-star skill levels. But you should accumulate many thousands of spare credits in this mission, so use them to raise operative skill levels.

Note, however, that you get only eight training programs, so choose your trainees wisely. Focus on raising already-high skill levels even higher. Some suggestions: Train up Stig in Mining, Slim in Laser, Hoshi or Kita in Electronics (for a future mission), Tami in Cleaning, Dean in Medi Prep, and Venus in Space Gas (or Power). Train up one Repair specialist (Nailer and Vasilios are good candidates for this) and one Maintenance specialist, too. In general, you want to have one highly-skilled expert and one backup expert (at least one star) in each skill.

Once trained, obviously, highly skilled operatives should be assigned primary and secondary jobs that correspond to their high skills.

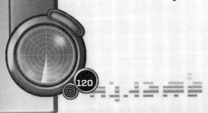

4-22. You have a good array of new defensive firepower. Put in some Manned Laser turrets so you can get them filled with purchased Argon Gas. This helps you get started in the next mission.

Boost Base Defense

You now have access to the powerful Manned Laser, plus you can place Automatic Lasers and the very potent upgrade of the Force Field Post called the Hi-Power Force Field Post. These are all very effective against the squads of disgusting Venusian Slugs that will slime up the base from time to time during this mission.

Of course, you have no access to Argon Gas deposits in this mission, and lasers don't work without Argon Gas. But you can buy Argon Gas canisters via Trade. They're relatively inexpensive at only 500 credits per 5-canister batch, so stockpile a lot of them and replenish the supply regularly. Spend!

Buy and place some Hover Mine Delivery Systems, too. Place them around the perimeter of the base for added defense against Slugs.

qwertyuiasl;zxcvbnm,.hjytfsz
To prepare for a future mission, place at least four Manned Lasers near the four monoliths southeast of your base.

Boost Base Power

This mission gives you access to Iridium Power Plants. These require Iridium Crystals to operate, but you can buy those via Trade, too. Put in a couple of power plants and buy 10 or 12 units of Iridium Crystals for fuel. These are expensive at 2000 credits per unit—but again, *spend!* You can't take it with you. (Not all of it, anyway.)

4-23. Consider adding some powerful Iridium Power Plants. Purchase Iridium Crystal fuel with all that extra cash you have on hand.

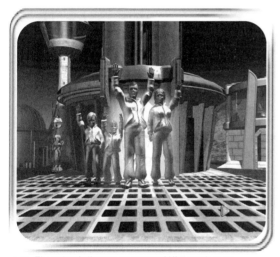

4-24. The galaxy's first 10-star resort! Nice work, team.

Check the Tourism Report for Clues

To get the coveted 10-star Tourism Rating, you must max-out the star rating of all four tourism sub-categories—Entertainment, Health & Hygiene, Food & Drink, and Safety. There's no real secret to this one, other than to give tourists what they want:

Entertainment. See "Expand Your Resort" above. The key is to provide the widest variety of recreation facilities possible.

Health & Hygiene. This is all about lots of Medi Bays, Personal Hygiene Pods, and Cleaning Posts. In this mission, you want to keep Candy, Tami, and Bhoomi cleaning all the time. Two of them should be assigned to Cleaning Posts in your tourist areas.

Food & Drink. Again, provide a variety. Place a few Mess Halls, Restaurants, Bars, and Luxury Bars. You need several of each to get the highest star rating in this category. The different tourist types (Dad, Mom, Boy, Girl) have different likes and dislikes regarding these facilities.

Safety. Protect the base, and especially the tourist areas, with plenty of Space Defense Shields. Keep your operatives happy (Nailer and Stig in particular) so you don't have any nasty worker-tourist incidents.

Check the tourism star ratings to see which category needs more work. Then keep adding Bio Domes full of the equipment and facilities needed to boost that rating. It's okay to spend wildly now, because you automatically start the next mission with 21,000 credits.

MISSION: THE HOST

Background

"Priority interrupt, code red. Strange energy fields are emanating from the surface of the planet. Taking you down there now..."

"Hello, humans. We are the Host. You are now our slaves. We will give you the plans for an intergalactic transporter. You will build this in the allotted time or you will all be killed. Resistance will be punished."

Main Objective

Build Transporter (acquire 50 Titanium units).

New Operatives

None

New Stuff Available

Host Transporter

4-25. Who are these guys? Better not fight them. Just be docile for now and build their contraption.

The Walkthrough

This mission can be short and sweet, especially if you have good miners (and you *should* by now). The Host gives you just 15 days to stockpile the 50 Titanium units you need to build the Host Transporter. Manned Lasers can hurt a Host, but don't try to fight—you'll just end up with dead colonists.

Find the Titanium (and Argon)

Pop down a couple of Lights in the extreme southeast corner of the map to find a black water lake and the Titanium deposits. Place an Argon Gas Rig on the water and a couple of Titanium Extractors near the deposits. Send Venus to the gas rig; send Stig and another good miner (Hoshi, Kita, or Slim) to run the extractors.

Keep Your People Happy (and Sane)

The Host are cruel taskmasters. If they sense psychological weakness in one of your colonists (say, Happiness or other Need bars in the red), a Host brain may drift over the poor fool's head and drive him insane. Then you must put the loony colonist either in the Detention Facility or send him/her to the Counseling Robot.

If folks go nuts, note that some respond better to one type of treatment than the other:

Send to Detention: Nailer, Stig, Kita, Hoshi, Billy Bob, Tami

Send to Counseling: Venus, Dean, Candy, Babette, Bhoomi

Send to Either Facility: Slim, Greg, Barbara, Vasilios, Nikolai

Success

As you mine Titanium, the Host Transporter is automatically built section by section. When droids transport the 50th Titanium unit to your warehouses, the mission is completed.

4-26. Okay, you built it for them. Now what?

MISSION: *REBELLION*

Background

Host: "Slave humans, your work is complete. Thank you for your hard work. My brethren are preparing to transport. I will remain here on this planet to oversee the process. Then I will kill you all."

Mr. Waterhouse: "We have found a frequency they can't detect. They must not be allowed to transport. Your base computer will brief you."

Base Computer: "Operative Nikolai will be smuggled down. He has plans for a new small-scale Cyrogenic Reanimation Unit that will help in defeating the Host life forms. Once inside the Transporter, they are powerless. Your are to build a Missile Silo and destroy the Transporter before the three Hosts can leave. The remaining Host will seek to prevent you from building the missile. You must defeat it."

Main Objective

Entire Host collective dead within 15 days!

New Operative

Nikolai rejoins your team.

New Stuff Available

- Cryogenic Reanimation Unit
- Missile Silo

The Walkthrough

At last—combat, man! But you need a fully loaded Missile Silo to blast the three Host creatures locked in their Transporter. The silo can't fire its missile until it has 20 Argon Gas canisters and 10 Electronics units. You also need Manned Laser turrets to destroy the fourth Host hovering overhead. Those require gas canisters, too.

All this means more Argon Gas Rig work for Venus, plus a new industry for your base: Electronics Fabrication. Hit Pause and take the following steps.

Don't place a Missile Silo until after you kill off the remaining Host! Otherwise, it simply drifts over the silo and destroys it.

Fire Up Two Argon Gas Rigs

You should have one in place already from the last mission. If not, add one now, and send Venus to work there. Then add a second one, and send Vasilios to work there. You'll need a lot of Argon Gas canisters to complete this mission.

Send Stig to Mine Silicon

You need Silicon for the Electronics Fabricator, and Stig is your best miner. You can also sell Silicon for the extra cash you need when it's time to reanimate your dead laser gunners later.

Place an Electronics Fabricator

This facility builds the advanced Electronics units you need for your Missile Silo. Send Hoshi or Kita (whoever has the highest Electronics skill) to work here. Meanwhile, train Nikolai up another skill level in Electronics, to three stars. Then send him to take over the job from the Japanese girl.

4-27. You need advanced electronics for you Missile Silo, so put in an Electronics Fabricator and assign Nikolai to work there.

Place Manned Lasers to Kill the Host

Only Manned Lasers hurt the remaining Host. If you haven't placed four turrets near the monoliths yet (and you *should* have if you're following our walkthrough), do so now. Then start sending your best Laser folks (Slim, Greg, Barbara, Hoshi, and Kita) to man them and open fire on the fourth Host.

As the Host destroy your Manned Laser turrets and kill your gunners, quickly replace the turrets and bring the dead gunners back via reanimation (see the next step).

4-28. Nail the brain when you can! From time to time it drifts off to target random colonists and drive them insane.

4-29. Place the Cryogenic Reanimation Unit near the Manned Lasers so you can recycle your gunners right back into a turret.

Buy a Reanimator

Put a Cryogenic Reanimation Unit in your base as close to the Manned Laser turrets as possible. It's expensive, but if necessary, sell off some of the stuff from your Tourist Fun Centers. You don't care about tourists as much now (although they *do* still bring in income to your base as they arrive).

Now when your gun crew dies off one by one when attacking the Host via Manned Lasers, bring them back quickly via the Cryogenic Reanimation Unit. Just select the unit and click the "Re-Animate Colonist" button. As soon as you place a new Manned Laser and warehouse droids arm it with Argon Gas canisters, send your re-animated colonists right back into the fray.

Some of your folks will die *several* deaths. Fun! But they always come back, thanks to the Cryogenic Reanimation Unit.

Monitor the Host

The Host occasionally drifts over your base and targets people for insanity. Until you finally manage to kill the big brainy beast with your Manned Lasers, follow its progress carefully, and quickly send mad workers to the appropriate rehabilitation facility.

(See the previous mission, **The Host**, for a list of which colonists respond better to the Detention Facility and which prefer the Counseling Robot.)

Build a Missile Silo

After (*not* before) you finally destroy the fourth Host, place a Missile Silo near the Host Transporter. Your warehouse droids load it up with Argon Gas (20 canisters) and Electronics (10 units) from your stockpiles. But the silo also needs 100 seconds of prep time; over it, you see the timer count down.

4-30. When the missile is ready, put the targeting cursor on the Alien Matter Transporter and click to fire away.

When the missile is ready, select the silo and click the Launch Missile button. Your cursor becomes a targeting reticule and you're asked to "Select target." Click the reticule on the Alien Matter Transporter and watch the final show!

4-31. Finally...Venus gets to head home.

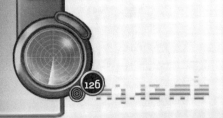

CHAPTER 5
MILITARY PATH: THE FAST PACED MISSIONS

5-1. The Military Path is all about fast-paced combat.

The Military Path takes you to a series of planets in the Aggerholm system. Your first two missions take place on a grim, volcanic world called Scrimgeour—a perfect name, somehow. From there you advance to a single engagement on harsh Farquharson, then move on to the lush jungle planet of Ealamoise for a pair of face-to-face confrontations with the Fribulan. The final two battles rage on Aggerholm.

qwertyuiopasdfghjkl-´zxcvbnm_´

PLANET: SCRIMGEOUR

MISSION: *IS ANYONE HEARING THIS? PLEASE HELP!*

Background

Base Computer: "A distress call has been picked up from one of our bases in the Aggerholm system. Their primary control systems have failed and they are under attack by a species of unknown origin. A rescue party must reach the base with a new central control core. The only operative fit, available, and within range is Venus Jones. The terrain is dangerous and infested with hostile life forms. Limited credits will be provided to boost defenses at the drop point to increase the probability of a successful mission."

Mr. Waterhouse: "This is Waterhouse here. I just got the message. This mission is top, and I mean *top* priority. Barbara Leechworth, company VP and one of our top people, was visiting when this happened and is now stranded down there. I want her lifted out."

Main Objective

Get Venus to the distressed base.

Operatives

Name: Venus

Mission Job: Power
Backup Job: Oxygen

Enemies

Rock Hoppers

Rock Hopper Queen

Military Hardware Available

- Automatic Laser
- High Power Force Field

The Walkthrough

This mission is not as tough as it may seem at first. Just keep in mind that you can place defensive structures up at the destination base, as well as at your drop point and along the route. You start with four Dogbots that cannot be replaced when destroyed, so use them carefully.

A total of 10 pregnant Rock Hopper Queens inhabit the area along the route you must follow to the distressed base.

Take a Peek Ahead

Hey, it's not cheating to Pause the game and look around. Especially when dark, creepy, bug-infested canyons loom up ahead. Place a Light on either side of the glowing volcano north of your defensive line. Trick: After placing the two Lights, click the Normal speed button and then *very quickly* click Pause again. This lets the Lights spread their glow over a wider area.

Now place one more Light as far south toward your defensive line as you can. Repeat the quick Normal/Pause double-click to let its glow spread. Wow! What do you see? Yes, those are five massive Rock Hopper Queens bursting with vicious Rock Hopper spawn.

Now click Normal speed again. The Rock Hopper spawn will immediately attack and destroy the Lights you just placed. But now you know what lies ahead.

5-2. Advance slowly, but surely, against the Rock Hopper Queens.

Opening Moves: Gas Up!

Put Venus to work at the Power console in the Bridge. She's going to sit tight until you can create a safe route for her to travel to the distressed base. You can move your Dogbots a few steps due west to center them on your defensive line, *but don't walk them beyond the perimeter yet.* Let your warehouse droids arm all four of your laser turrets first.

After your defense fights off a swarm or two of Rock Hoppers, it's time to begin your march northward. But first, open the Trade Controls and buy at least 40 units of Argon Gas (50 or 60 is a safer bet). You'll place a lot of laser turrets that expend a lot of Argon Gas canisters in this mission.

Send in the Dogs

The basic strategy is to move systematically from one Rock Hopper Queen to the next, wiping out all 10 of them while regularly checking on the distressed base and adding new lasers and Force Field Posts when necessary. Again, Venus stays behind, running the drop-point facility and keeping her basic needs satisfied. Your four Dogbots do the heavy work, fighting together with Automatic Lasers that you place along the route.

The direct path leads due north past the volcano, and then east toward the distressed base. But you want to destroy all five of the Rock Hopper Queens near your starting base first. So target the Queen to the northwest first, and eliminate Queens and their minions one by one across your front to the northeast.

How to Advance Against Hoppers

The basic movement pattern works like this. First, inch your Dogbots forward a couple of steps—not too far, though. (Dogbots can't fire while moving, so don't send them on long treks.) Keep the dogs well within range of your loaded Automatic Lasers, because when a Rock Hopper swarm hits, you need more than just four laser guns to keep the beasts at bay.

Place a Light amongst the Dogbots to see ahead and extend the range of all lasers. Don't put the Light *ahead* of your Dogbots, though, because the Rock Hoppers likely will destroy it before you can gun them all down. Place another Automatic Laser turret up near your Dogbots, too. Wait for droids to arm this new turret with Argon Gas canisters, then inch the Dogbots forward again and place another Light amongst them, then a new turret, and so on.

5-3. Let your Dogbots blaze the trail to the distressed base.

Past the Medical Dome

Repeat this slow, methodical movement northeast, blasting all five Queens in the area. When you nail the fifth Queen, the swarms stop for a while and you can seek a safe path through the lava field. At one point you have to cross a little lava that causes damage, but it's a very short stretch.

Continue north past a Small Bio Dome on the right with a Medi Bay inside. (This will be useful for Venus later when she crosses the lava, too.) Then veer northwest and fight your way up the passage to the sixth Rock Hopper Queen.

Check the Destination Base

You should be dropping in extra lasers and posts at the base under attack in the northeast.

Two More Pairs of Queens

Stay patient! Don't rush your Dogbots too far ahead out of supporting turret range, or Hopper spawn will overwhelm them. After the sixth Queen, move slowly northwest, then turn east and place two more Automatic Lasers just ahead of your Dogbots. Two more Queens block the passage leading east. Zap them!

If you've still got at least two Dogbots, you're in very good shape here. Only two more Queens remain on the route up ahead. Place two more Automatic Lasers up ahead, wait for them to arm with Argon Gas, then push your dogs a couple of steps closer to get within range of the last two Queens. When you exterminate them, the rest of the way is clear to the destination base.

Send the Dogbots forward to help the base defenses hold off Rock Hopper swarms emerging from the Forbidden Zone south of the base.

Send in Venus

Back at the drop point facility, get Venus ready for a long walk. Top off her overall Happiness by sending her to the equipment that satisfies needs—shower, bed, Counseling Robot, Mess Hall, and Rowing Machine. Then send her up the route to the Bio Dome with the Medi Bay. She takes damage walking across the lava, but a Medi Bay session once she arrives cures the hurt.

Now guide her northwest through the passage, then east toward the distressed base. When she arrives at the base Bridge dome, you've successfully completed the mission.

MISSION: *RESCUE*

Background

"An evac team is close by, but has been put on hold by Miss Leechworth as the company's Iridium extraction operation is not complete. The base is now operational but is very badly damaged. If the Iridium is to be collected before we are overrun by the aliens, then much repair work will need to be carried out."

Main Objective

Acquire 10 Iridium Crystals.

New Operatives

Name: Barbara Leechworth
Mission Job: Scavenging
Backup Job: Oxygen

Name: Greg Chesterton
Mission Job: Mining
Backup Job: None

Name: Nailer McBride
Mission Job: Repair
Backup Job: Cleaning

Name: Mr. Zhang
Mission Job: None
Backup Job: None

Name: Slim
Mission Job: Oxygen
Backup Job: Mining

New Enemies

5.3 Metaflaxus Plant (spawns Burnflies)

New Military Hardware

- Dog Bot Post
- Force Field Post

The Walkthrough

This mission presents a double challenge. You have military objectives, of course. But you also need to develop a viable base from scratch.

After the Forbidden Zone is opened, place a couple Lights to the south and southwest. You see the Iridium deposits—and a couple of fat, pulsating Rock Hopper Queens ready to spew their spawn at your mining operation.

But before you engage the enemy, you have some basic colony-building tasks to perform. Hit Pause and do all of the preparation work outlined in the next few steps.

Secure the Perimeters!

Primary attacks come from the south, but Rock Hoppers will swoop in from the west, too. Put in a line of Force Field Posts across the opening to the west; be sure to push the line out a short distance past the small Titanium deposit. Then place two Automatic Lasers behind the line. You want to protect the base, but you also want to keep the Titanium area secure, too, for the mining you'll soon do.

Now place more Automatic Lasers to the south—you need a total of about four or five turrets here. String a line of Force Field Posts across the canyon opening south of the lasers.

Trade for Critical Goods

Open your Trade Controls window. Buy 15-20 Argon Gas canisters for your early laser needs and just 5-10 units of Base Nutrients to get started with your colonist food needs.

5-4. Buy plenty of Argon Gas canisters for your laser turrets.

Build Your Base

Iridium mining is expensive—5000 for the Scavenger Bunker alone!—and the deposits are in dangerous Rock Hopper territory. So before you send miners down there, establish the colony and get some income to cover the costs.

Although, you may not have enough credits to do everything in this section, keep the game on Pause for now and do the following base-building steps in order of importance:

1. Assign Barbara to the Oxygen desk and Venus to the Power desk.

2. Put an Oxygen Plant north of the base.

3. Install a Titanium Extractor beside the Titanium deposits to the west. (We put this step early because you need the Titanium to generate some extra income.) Assign Greg, your best miner, to work there.

4. Your facilities, defense, and mining equipment will take damage (sometimes significant) from Hopper attacks, so put in an Engineering Repair Station and assign Nailer to work there.

5. Add a Small or Medium Bio Dome adjacent to your bridge and put in a Mess Hall, Personal Hygiene Pod, Social Area, and Cleaning Post. Assign Nailer to this, but switch it to his secondary job. (His Repair work is much more important.)

6. Put four beds in the Small Bio Dome up the corridor to the northeast, then add two more in the Medium Bio Dome near the warehouse area. Unfortunately, you have three colonist who have Sleep as a special need—Nailer, Slim, and Mr. Zhang. Give them beds in the closer, Small Bio Dome. Assign the two farthest beds to Greg and Barbara, who have the least need for Sleep.

7. Add a Medi Bay in case your miners get attacked. Put Barbara on the Medi Prep console long enough to prep the bay, then move her back to Oxygen.

8. Later, when you get some income from Titanium mining, add some amenities like a Sauna or Jacuzzi (everyone likes these), a Disco (keep Barbara off this), a Running Machine (keep Slim off this), and a Combat Arena (Greg and Slim are neutral on this).

Keep Mining the Titanium to the West

We mentioned this in the last step, but feel it's important to reiterate it here. That Titanium brings a good price on the open market, so have Greg mine it all up. When the deposit is depleted, sell off the Titanium Extractor.

qwertyuiasl;zxcvbnm,.hjytfsa

Keep your Argon Gas stockpile at about 20 canisters. Don't forget to check it regularly (and your Base Nutrients stock, too) in the Trade Controls window.

Extend the Defensive Perimeter South

Unless you can afford a couple of Dogbots (very expensive at 2000 apiece), you must move incrementally southwest toward the Iridium deposits. A big Queen sits just south of the canyon entrance, guarding the Iridium west of her. Put in a pair of lasers near the canyon rock, wait for them to get armed, then drop in a Light next to them to reveal the Queen to their targeting systems.

5-5. Find the first Iridium deposits just inside the south canyon entrance—and guarded by a Queen.

Don't forget your western perimeter! Add an extra Automatic Laser or two and more Force Field Posts when you can afford it.

Collect the Crystals

After your guns pop the first Queen and her minions, put in two more lasers just south of the Iridium deposit, drop in another Light next to them, and then, finally, put in your Scavenger Bunker to start collecting Iridium Crystals. Order Barbara (the only one other than Venus with Scavenging skill) to work the bunker, and put Slim in her place at the Oxygen desk.

The first deposits aren't enough to provide the 10-unit requirement of Iridium Crystals, so your Scavenger Robot will start moving southwest to find more deposits. Be sure you stay out in front of it with your laser emplacements! You do *not* want to lose that robot.

Torch the Metaflaxus

From time to time a Metaflaxus plant will spring up, full of deadly Burnflies that will start spreading seeds for more Metaflaxus. When you see one of these plants, try to get a Weeding Post near it and send Nailer (with his 3-star Weeding skill) to work from it. But do this only if the area is well covered by laser turrets. You don't want to lose Nailer and his Repair skill to a Rock Hopper rush.

Root Out the Queens

Most of the Rock Hopper Queens lurk to the south and southwest of the Iridium deposits. You can aggressively push your lasers inch by inch into their dens and wipe them out. If you get enough cash to add some Dogbots to this extermination, go ahead and do it. Remember to place Lights by laser turrets to increase their range. (They can't hit what they can't see.)

You don't have to eliminate every Rock Hopper Queen in the region to win this mission, but it certainly helps to wipe out the three Queens down in the southwest caverns. This secures that area for your Scavenger Robot.

PLANET: FARQUHARSON
MISSION: *MOONSHAKER*

Background

"Farquharson is a small and unstable planet rich in the Pharmaceutical-bearing Cylincsus plant-form. Indigenous to the planet are the Hyracsus, large beasts that feed off these plants—quite stupid, but with a deadly earth tremor attack capable of damage to a wide area. A consignment of new military hardware has been made available for your use."

Main Objective

Acquire 10 Pharmaceutical units.

New Operatives

Venus takes Barbara, Slim, Greg, and Mr. Zhang to Farquharson, and adds two new operatives.

Name: Hoshi
Mission Job: Pharmaceutical
Backup Job: Power

Name: Kita
Mission Job: Pharmaceutical
Backup Job: Repair

New Enemies

Hyracsus

Lava Beetle

Protean Worm

Protean Worm Mother

New Military Hardware

- ◄▐⁻ Soldier Post
- ◄▐⁻ Military Robotics Factory
- ◄▐⁻ Manned Laser

The Walkthrough

This wild, wooly mission sends alien attackers at your base from all directions. You start with some basic colony facilities plus a Military Robotics Factory, which can produce the powerful robotic Soldiers you desperately need in this mission.

Unfortunately, you need both Titanium and advanced electronics to build Soldiers, and both are very expensive. So you'll have to play defense with Automatic and Manned Turrets until you can mine your own Titanium and sell enough to buy Electronics units.

Set Up Your Base

You should be getting the hang of building an efficient base by now, so we'll just highlight some key points:

- Buy Argon Gas canisters. Keep a total of 20 or so in stock, replenishing when necessary.
- Beef up your defenses, adding an extra Automatic Laser turret on each side. Also put two at the edge of the lava field to the north to protect your Lava Power Plant from wandering Lava Beetles and those annoying, spitting Protean Worms.
- Add a Light and at least two Automatic Laser turrets near the Titanium deposits just northwest of the base. When the guns are armed, place a Titanium Extractor and get Greg to work there.
- Place a Pharmaceutical Extractor in your base and make it the primary job of both Hoshi and Kita. As soon as possible, add a second extractor. Rotate Hoshi, Kita, and Barbara at these two jobs.

You need two Titanium and two Electronics units to manufacture each Soldier.

Build Soldier Robots

You start with three empty Soldier Posts. When you've mined enough Titanium and can afford to buy some Electronics via trade, send Venus to the Military Robotics Factory and start cranking out Soldiers. These will be *very* important units in this mission, because your Automatic Turrets are too vulnerable against the Protean Worms and the occasional massive Hyracsus.

When the first Soldier emerges, keep him near the factory so he can help defend it against worm and other attacks. Do the same with the second Soldier. When the third Soldier emerges, send two around the base to its northwest corner, where most of the Hyracsus attacks will come.

5-6. These new Soldier robots can make things much easier for you in this mission.

Find and Light the Cylincsus

Your Pharmaceutical Extractor droids (you should have two working by now) cannot find Cylincsus in the dark. If you don't light up the plants, the droids see nothing. So once you find a couple of Cylincus patches, keep dropping Lights into their midst. Worms, Hoppers, and Hyracsus will smash the Lights. Just put in new ones.

Eventually, when you find the big Cylincus patch west of the base, you can send out a Soldier or two to defend the Lights. Again, if the Lights get destroyed, simply replace them again and again until you have your 10 units of Pharmaceuticals.

Play Defense

One strategy is to send your Soldiers out to nail the immobile Protean Worm Mothers, thereby eliminating the spawning of their offspring, the Protean Worms. (The in-game tips mention this approach.) But this runs the risk of isolating your slow Soldiers far from your base; the Worm Mothers are spread widely over the map.

So we recommend keeping your Soldiers home to guard the base against the approach of the powerful Hyracsus. In the long run, these huge monsters can cause more trouble than the annoying worms.

Consider putting in one or two Manned Laser turrets at the points where you face the most pressure from alien attacks. Slim is very skilled (two stars) in Laser operation, so put him aboard.

Watch for the Hyracsus!

The thundering Hyracsus damages all structures (including Lights and laser turrets) within a large radius when it slams the ground. So the key is to find these slow-moving beasts well before they reach your base or exterior rigs. You can hear them coming—the screen literally shakes when one approaches.

Watch and listen. When you get an idea of its approach route, pop some Lights in the area to find the creature, then send a couple of your Soldiers out to intercept the Hyracsus before it can reach your base.

With two Pharmaceutical Extractors working, you can meet your quota quickly. Remember: Just keep lighting up the Cylincsus areas.

5-7. The Protean Worms are bad enough, but the massive Hyracsus can topple your entire base if you don't stop him.

PLANET: EALAMOISE
MISSION: *THE FRIBULAN*

Background

"We have been set a target for the amount of Titanium we are to stockpile. The Fribulan have already started mining the resource and are in full production. Military action is obviously a possibility, but tactical data suggests this would be a disastrous option."

Main Objective

Acquire 50 Titanium units.

New Operatives

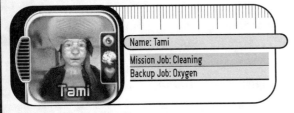

Name: Tami

Mission Job: Cleaning
Backup Job: Oxygen

Enemies

Acidwing

Gorilloid

Marsh Fairy

Marsh Fairy Hatcher

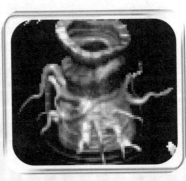

Fribulan Spitter Rodent (Diseased!)

New Military Hardware

- Hover Mine Delivery System
- Military Radar

The Walkthrough

Wow, this is a huge map, and it's crawling with bad things. Most areas are choked with vegetation, too—including the zone around your colony base. The planet fairly bristles with Titanium deposits; however, you can win by staying right in your own backyard. In fact, if you go Magellan and circumnavigate in search of deposits beyond the big one just north of your base, you will run into some very nasty creatures that will destroy your puny search party.

> Don't put an Argon Gas Rig into the nearby black water swamp—not even after Slim destroys the Spitter with his Manned Laser. The Fribulan, Marsh Fairies, and other destructive creatures will cross the lake regularly during the mission, making it almost impossible to maintain a rig unless you push your defenses west.

First Steps

- Put Venus directly into the Nutrient Harvester waiting for you, for gosh sake! You need to clear the vegetation around the base so you can put in more Bio Domes for your bedrooms and other expansion.

- Send Slim right to the Manned Laser turret already in place just north of the base.

- Order Barbara to the Medi Prep desk to prep the three Medi Bays you inherit.

- Assign Hoshi and Kita to Power and Oxygen. Have them both back up Slim on the Manned Laser with their secondary jobs.

- Install a Cleaning Post and put Tami to work there, with Power as her secondary job.

5-8. Your primary focus should be on securing and then mining the Titanium deposit just north of your base.

- Put in a Titanium Extractor by the Titanium deposits just north of the base. When Greg arrives, have him work there immediately. You don't want the Fribulan to get *too* big a jump on you.

- It will be a while before you get room for a bedroom Bio Dome, so pack three beds into the far corner of your Large Bio Dome for the colonists with Sleep special needs: Nailer, Mr. Zhang, and Slim. The others can go sleepless for a while until you can clear away some brush for expansion.

- Place a few Automatic Laser turrets around the base walls to zap the March Fairies (look like flying jellyfish) that drift in to attack from time to time.

- Add a Warehouse on the northeast end of your warehouse area.

Layer Your Security

As you build a little income, spend it on security. Keep your Argon Gas canister supply at 20-plus at all times, and put in more Automatic Turrets when you can. Consider adding one more Manned Laser near the shore of the black water lake to the west, with one of the Japanese girls in the cab. Keep lining the lake with laser turrets. Replace them each time one is destroyed by Fribulan or Marsh Fairy attacks.

Slowly push out your defensive perimeter north as the mission proceeds, dropping in lots of Automatic Turrets and a few Hover Mine Delivery Systems. This creates a nice buffer for your Titanium Extractors. It's also important later in the mission when the Gorilloids start lurching down from the north.

Keep Your Focus on Mining

Ealamoise is an interesting planet full of beautiful and deadly creatures. Stay away from them, okay? Resist the urge to push into the central valley just west of your base area. The in-game tips suggest you can control this valley and thus disrupt the Fribulan mining effort, and that's not a bad idea if you don't mind expending great energy and spreading yourself and your resources thin.

However, there is enough Titanium in that one deposit north of your base to extract the 50 units you need to win this mission. So the simple solution is to focus your full attention on pushing your defenses north to secure that area, and then...

Add a Second Titanium Extractor

If you haven't done so already, get another mining rig up near the Titanium deposits as soon as the northern area is secure. With two rigs running, you should keep ahead of the Fribulan pace in the mining race. Send Nailer up to do this job, but keep Repair as his secondary job.

qwertyuiasl;zxcvbnm,.hjytfsz

> Keep Greg and Nailer happy! Happy miners are hardworking miners. So give the boys what they love during their off-work hours. In particular, Greg loves the Jacuzzi, and Nailer loves the Combat Arena.

Rodent Infestation

Mr. Waterhouse reports a "few slight glitches" in the military systems on Day 2. Your lasers won't fire for a short while, but hang in there. When a swarm of disease-carrying Rodents overwhelms the base, most of your colonists get infected.

Fortunately, your three prepped Medi Bays are stocked with Pharmaceuticals. Send infected colonists there to be cured, and keep Barbara prepping them after each use. You can get everybody cured pretty quickly, and soon the targeting systems reactivate and stay on for the rest of the mission.

Chew Up the Scenery

Keep your Nutrient Extractor hacking down trees around the colony. Remember that you can select the area for harvesting by clicking on the harvester robot. Clear the area southeast of the base first. This area remains relatively unmolested by alien attackers during the mission, so it's the perfect area for adding a Medium Bio Dome.

This dome can be your bunkhouse, holding all nine beds. (You can move the three beds you placed earlier. Just click on a bed and select Move Building, then click on the spot where you want to move it.) Be sure to add some Airlocks for access.

Add More Warehouse Space

Your 50 units of Titanium take up space, so you want a couple more Warehouses. But the area is overgrown, and the Manned Laser blocks one prime warehouse spot. Once you've got your Bio Dome placed in the southeast, you can direct your harvester robot to clear the plants around the warehouse area. When you have enough credits, place a new Manned Laser further north and sell off the turret blocking your warehouse expansion.

Place Lights to Distract Gorilloids

Big honking Gorilloids stomp down from the north at random intervals later in the mission. Each one of these big guys can, as the manual puts it, "use its sonic roar weapon to great destructive effect." Just a few Gorilloid howls can knock out your entire defensive grid, unless you've spent time layering it as we suggested earlier.

You really want to keep these fellows away from your Titanium Extractors. Here's a tip: Gorilloids are very distracted by Lights. If one of these big aliens starts roaring and blasting your laser turrets to Smithereens (and we're not referring to the rock band), start surrounding it with Lights. As the beast turns to "roar" them to pieces, your remaining lasers can slowly wear him down. Plus, you can drop in additional lasers behind your front line defenses.

5-g. The Gorilloid roar is brutal and deadly. Distract him with Lights while your lasers do their work.

Eventually, your pair of Titanium Extractors will outpace the Fribulan, and win the mining race.

MISSION: *SPINEWEED*

Background

Venus: "Well, the good news is that we beat the Frib to the punch. Bad news is they are not happy about it. They've let loose another of their living machines—giant Spineweed; part metal, part organic. It's kind of a killer vegetable, and scans show its course is straight towards us. The lasers don't even scratch it. Computer, any ideas?"

Base Computer: "Yes, Venus, data is coming in now. Lasers are ineffective, but use of the new Cluster Bomb should retard its progress. To eradicate the weed completely, however, the Fribulan Mother must be destroyed, as this provides all control for the plant form. A delivery of Sentinels is en route, and should soon be available for your use to help combat the Acidwings that are preventing access to the Fribulan base."

Main Objective

Destroy the Fribulan base.

New Operatives

Candy rejoins your team.

New Enemies

Spineweed

Fribulan Mother

New Military Hardware

- ⊞ Cluster Bomb
- ⊞ Sentinel Post
- ⊞ Sentinel Patrol Marker

The Walkthrough

Here's a classic military campaign. Your goal: Destroy the enemy base. Your method: Spend time fortifying your own base while amassing a powerful assault force. Acidwings prowl the approach routes to the Fribulan Mother, and the unstoppable Spineweed is coming. Fun!

Several routes lead across the map from your colony in the southeast corner, up to the swamp in the northwest corner where the Mother resides. We like the most direct one—the southern route that runs along the bottom of the map, then north.

Early Phase

But wait. You have *lots* to do before you get to the phase where you actually launch your attack. As the mission opens, you are vastly outnumbered by the forces of evil. Plus, you don't have the Sentinels yet, and you can't really tangle with a flight of Acidwings without them.

Again, by now you should be plenty familiar with basic colony housekeeping—how to keep your workers happy and hardworking, and how to defend your base. The early phase is all about gearing up your means of production. Here are a few steps to take in the early going:

5-10. Cluster Bombs are the only weapon you have that can stop the relentless Spineweed advance. Place several west and north of your base.

- Place Cluster Bombs along the base perimeter. When the Spineweed comes, these mortar-like guns will eliminate the encroachment.

- Place Hover Mine Delivery Systems along the base perimeter, too. The Acidwings don't attack your base as a rule, but if they wander close, the mines can drive them back. Hover Mines are good against the Fribulan who try to infiltrate your base, as well.

- Keep mining that Titanium! You need *lots* and *lots* of credits to build an army of Soldiers and Sentinels. Run two Titanium Extraction rigs with Greg and Nailer.

- Keep Slim, Hoshi, and Kita in a trio of Manned Lasers arranged to the west and north of the base. These powerful lasers are particularly effective against the nonstop stream of Fribulan foot soldiers.

- *Important:* When you get a chance, get a Training Pod and train the three teens up a level on their Laser skill. You need all the defensive firepower you can get in the early going.

- Place an Argon Gas Rig in the black water lake next to your warehouse area and assign Venus to work there. Producing your own gas saves a lot of cash in the long run. Be sure to surround the rig with Automatic Lasers and Lights.

Middle Phase

Once you've got a well-layered defense around your base, it's time for your offensive buildup. Your Titanium mining brings in good credits, so do the following:

- Build a force of 8 to 10 Soldiers, placing their posts near your base. Add in a few Dogbots, too—they're cheaper, but they still provide some decent firepower. Perhaps more importantly, they draw some fire away from your Soldiers when you go on the march.

- Of course, don't forget your colonists, either. In particular, keep your miner (Greg), your gas rig girl (Venus), and your three teen Laser gunners chipper and willing to work long hours.

- After you get a strong squad of Soldiers and Dogbots, start saving up for Sentinels. They're very pricey at 6000 apiece, but you need three or four of them patrolling your route to the Fribulan Mother; they keep the Acidwings at bay.

- Place Sentinel Posts near your base. You don't want to endanger the Sentinel; when the post goes, the Sentinel goes, too. Instead, place Sentinel Patrol Markers along the route when the time comes.

- Be sure you have two Engineering Repair Facilities and two workers with Repair skill assigned. It's good to have a couple of repair droids at work when you make your move across hostile territory.

Endgame

Just go for it! March your entire force of Soldiers and Dogbots straight to the Fribulan Mother. To do so, select all of your troops, then scroll the map to the Mother and click right next to her.

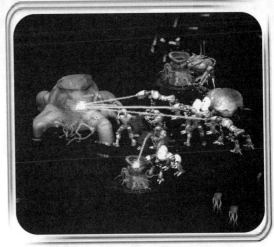

Follow the progress and place Sentinel Patrol Markers every few seconds so your Sentinels are nearby to provide air support. (Enemies will blast the markers quickly, but just keep planting new ones ahead of your marching Soldiers.) Your troops will take damage en route, but don't stop and fight back anywhere. If you have two Repair Facilities (as we suggested earlier), the two repair droids hover overhead and repair units as they march. Just let the Soldiers walk all the way to the Fribulan Mother, where they will open fire on her.

5-11. Send your squad of Soldiers and Dogbots directly at the Fribulan Mother. A slow, methodical fight through her minions is doomed to fail.

As few as four Soldiers can take out the Mother if the repair droids stay active. However, if you send in a force of 8 to 10 Soldiers, your odds of destroying her before losing all your troops are very, very good.

MISSION: BETRAYAL ON AGGERHOLM

Background

"We are to create and defend a beachhead in the marked zone. From that point we are to complete construction of missiles at each of the silos. At no point are we to fire any of the missiles. No evac details are currently scheduled."

Main Objective

Complete 3 missiles within 25 days.

New Operatives

Vasilios rejoins your team.

New Enemies

Protoraptor

New Military Hardware

- Missile Silo
- Cryogenic Reanimation Unit

The Walkthrough

This is a straightforward mission. To build the three missiles in the Missile Silos you require a lot of Argon Gas units—60 to be exact. Protoraptors will throw wave after wave of attacks at your base. So if you rely on your laser turrets for defense, you will constantly deplete the Argon Gas supply. The key to success, then, is to develop a force of robotic military units to counter the protoraptor attack waves and destroy their breeding pods.

The Robot Strategy

You start with four Soldier robots. Use the hefty credit account you start with to invest in at least six Dogbots. Send a couple of the dogs to the northwest corner of the map to kill the protoraptor breeding pods there. Position the rest of the robots on the eastern perimeter of your base.

As you proceed with the following steps, keep the eastern side of the base secure. Add more Dogbots as you can afford it. Then send a hunter-killer squad of four Dogbots/Soldiers (any combination you like) heading east. Plant Lights ahead of their progress as you direct them to seek and destroy protoraptor breeding pods. The more pods you kill, the fewer protorapters spawn and attack.

5-12. Every breeding pod you destroy means fewer protoraptor rushes. Send out a "seek and destroy" squad of robots.

Develop Your Base

Okay, no more hand-holding. You know what your people need. Hit Pause and give it to them. Create a thriving base with basic amenities and a good cross-section of entertainment facilities. Make sure everybody has beds. Add some Solar Power Plants, two more Warehouses, and a Training Pod. And don't forget that Disco for your teenagers!

Next, attend to base security. Place a Manned Laser beside the Missile Silos and assign Slim to it (when he steps off the shuttle later) as soon as it's armed with Argon. Very important: Add an Engineering Repair Facility to be manned by Nailer! Your base and robots will take a lot of damage from protoraptor attacks, so you need this facility to keep things functioning in the rough stretches ahead.

When you're finished placing everything, keep the game on Pause for the next several steps.

Find Black Water

You need a lot of Argon Gas, and unlike in other missions, here you have to produce it all yourself—Argon Gas cannot be purchased via trade. Each Missile Silo requires 20 canisters, and of course you need plenty of gas for your base defenses, too.

Find the bubbling black water lake northeast of the base and place two Argon Gas Rigs on it. Assign Venus and Vasilios to do the honors. Put at least four Automated Laser turrets around the rigs, though. Protoraptors will start to prowl very soon.

5-13. You must provide your own Argon Gas in this mission, so place two rigs in the black water.

Mine Silicon for Electronics

You also need 10 units of advanced Electronics per missile, and you can't buy these via trade, either. So you need an Electronics Fabrication facility—two, actually, if you want to beat the mission timer by a safe margin—with Hoshi and Kita working them. Place both facilities right next to your warehouse area to reduce travel time for the warehouse droids when they deliver silicon.

That's right: you can't fabricate Electronics without pure Silicon. Guess what? You can't buy *that* either. So you have to mine your own Silicon. Fortunately, there's a large Silicon deposit southwest of the base. Put two Silicon Extractors next to it, and send Greg run one. You need Nailer working feverishly in the repair facility, so use the Training Pod to teach Mr. Zhang the Mining skill, then send him to the second extractor.

⌁⌁⌁⌁⌁⌁⌁⌁⌁⌁⌁⌁⌁⌁⌁⌁⌁⌁⌁⌁⌁⌁⌁⌁⌁⌁⌁⌁⌁⌁

While waiting for the first loads of Silicon for the Electronics Fabricators, train both Kita and Hoshi in Electronics at the Training Pod. Train up Vasilios and Venus in Space Gas, too.

Trade Lasers for Dogs

As you gain income, buy Dogbots and put them by laser turrets, then sell off the turrets. Why? Because the fewer lasers you have sucking away Argon Gas from your rig, the faster your Missile Silos get gas canisters to build their missiles!

Kill off as many of the protoraptor breeding pods in the mission area as you can.

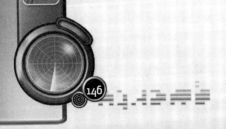

MISSION: *A Bad Thing*

Background

"The raptors must be eradicated and all breeding pods destroyed or scavenged and processed via the new alien storage facility. Scans report the presence of an Orox Guardian in the vicinity and deep space listeners have detected several more in transit. The missiles are not to be used and are still locked out."

Main Objectives

- Destroy all protoraptor breeding pods.
- Kill any protoraptors spawned.

New Operatives

Babette rejoins your team.

New Enemies

Orox

New Military Hardware

None

The Walkthrough

This is a very tough mission if you approach it conventionally—that is, if you march your Soldiers slowly from one pod nest to another, seeking to wipe out the protoraptors and pods. And it's even *tougher* if you didn't destroy all the protoraptor pods you could reach in the last mission.

But we have a couple of tactics that can help make things quite a bit easier. In general, the overall strategy is this: the quicker you destroy pods, the faster you eliminate the horror of facing endless swarms of protoraptors.

The Pause that Refreshes

First off, know that you'll spend most of this mission with the game Paused. If you find that tactic to be wimpy, then we dare you to complete this mission without using it. (Pardon us while we snicker at the very thought.) Okay, hit Pause.

Sell Off *All* Military Robots

This may seem like an odd thing to do, but you'll see why it's important in a minute. Your credit account starts high in this mission, but you can use all the extra credits you can get. Go ahead, sell off *all* of your Soldiers and Dogbots. You're going to buy new stuff shortly. Don't worry about credits lost to depreciation. Ideally, you want to end up with more than 48,000 credits so you can buy a full complement of Soldiers (12 at 4000 apiece) later. But any nice, high number of credits will do.

> *Remember that to sell off a Soldier or Dogbot, you must click the "Sell Base Structures" button, and then click on the unit's post, not on the unit itself.*

Keep Rigs Running

You will need more Electronics and Argon Gas canisters for extra missiles in the next mission, so keep your Argon Gas Rig and Electronics Fabricator active.

Beef Up Base Defenses

Selling off military robots weakens your base defense, so add four or five Hover Mine Delivery Systems along the eastern perimeter of your base. Add a few more Automatic Lasers, too. You don't want to lose base structures while you're off gallivanting in search of pods.

Wipe Out Visible Pod Nests

Still Paused, we trust? Now scroll around the map. Several protoraptor pod nests are visible via the glow of Photocyn mushrooms. How convenient! Let's go kill them before they spawn more of the vicious little beasts.

> You can place a Scavenger Bunker near some of the smaller nests and try to scavenge a few pods for sale. This is a risky but viable way to make a few thousand extra credits.

The trick: Place new Soldiers right in the middle of each protoraptor pod nest. The robots attack pods and destroy them quickly. You can place up to 12 Soldier Posts at any one time, so you can hit several (if not all) of the visible nests at the same time. If the nest is small—five or fewer pods—place just one Soldier Post. If the nest is bigger—the one in the Silicon deposit in the northwest corner of the map, for example—place two Soldier Posts. Place Soldier Posts in as many nests as you can afford Soldiers.

5-14. Some protoraptor pod nests are lit by Photocyn mushrooms. Others, like this one, you'll have to find by placing Lights.

Pods ready to spawn protoraptors will pulsate and have a protrusion at the top.

Important: Soldiers will attack protoraptors before they attack pods. So if the mushroom glow reveals any of the toothy beasts lurking nearby, add a Hover Mine Delivery System in the nest, too. Hover mines are particularly effective against protoraptors. You want to wipe out the slavering monsters and get your Soldiers focusing their fire on the pods as soon as possible, before any spawning occurs.

5-15. Place Soldiers right in the midst of pod nests. And do it quickly, before the pods spawn protoraptors.

Sell Quickly Afterwards

Once your Soldier Posts and Hover Mine Delivery Systems are all placed, click the Normal speed button. Monitor the pod slaughter in each nest. When all pods are eliminated from a nest, immediately sell off the Soldier Post(s) in that nest. The sooner you sell, the less depreciation you suffer in the sale.

When all visible nests are empty, hit Pause again and sell off any remaining Soldier Posts.

Keep Your Base in Order

Check back on your colonists and their needs from time to time. Run down your personnel list and do a little micromanaging if necessary, sending people where they need to go. You don't want insane operatives running amok while you're out battling the forces of evil.

Light Up Hidden Nests

Check your "pod/protoraptor counter" in the upper-left corner of the screen. It indicates you've killed less than half the protoraptors and pods in the mission. Next step: Find the hidden pods.

Still Paused, start placing Lights, extending the visible area outward from your base. Be systematic in your placement. Any dark patch could hide a nasty nest of pods.

Very important: A very powerful Orox guards one very large nest in the north-central part of the map. *Leave this nest for last!* We have a trick that can make the Orox battle easier, but it works only if all other nests are scoured clean of pods first.

> *If you run out of credits while searching for pod nests, sell off Lights you've placed.*
> *If you've kept the game on Pause, you get a full credit refund!*

When you find a nest, place a Soldier Post or two (depending on the nest size) as close to the breeding pods as possible. Again, if protoraptors are about, drop in a Hover Mine Delivery System, too. Keep finding nests and placing Soldiers until you run out of credits, then click Normal speed and let your robots wipe out the pods.

Sell off Soldiers and repeat this process until you've revealed the entire map and the only remaining nest with pods is the huge central one with the Orox guard.

Wipe Out the Orox-Guarded Nest

Here's the secret to which we alluded earlier. Actually, it's not so secret—it's stated right on the screen, in fact. If you move your cursor over the mission objective in the upper left corner, you see your goal is this: "All Protoraptors & Eggs Killed." Notice it says absolutely nothing about an Orox.

Place a few Lights to illuminate the big Orox-guarded nest of pods, then plunk down a few Hover Mine Delivery Systems near the Orox to distract him. Next, place as many Soldier Posts as you can afford in the southern half of the nest—the side furthest away from the Orox. Place a full squad of 12 if you have the credits!

Hit Normal speed. The Orox busies himself roaring warnings and blasting the Hover Mine Delivery Systems. Meanwhile your massed Soldiers wipe out every pod in the nest. When the last pod pops, guess what? You win. Unless, of course, some stray protoraptors still prowl the darkness.

> You'll have to battle the Orox in the next mission. But it's much better to fight him without hordes of protoraptors ripping up your troops while you fight. Plus you'll have even stronger military robots in "Death or Glory."

5-16. Distract the Orox with Lights and Hover Mine Delivery Systems, then deploy your Soldiers to massacre the pods in the large central nest.

If you clean out the Orox-guarded nest and the mission still doesn't end, that means pods and/or protoraptors still live somewhere. (The "protoraptor counter" will indicate enemies remain.) Sell off all Soldiers and start scanning the map for the stragglers or pods you've overlooked. Ignore the howling Orox. Place Lights in every patch of darkness. Sooner or later you'll find the last protoraptors or pods. Place Soldier Posts and wipe them out.

5-17. All pods must die! (Or be scavenged!)

MISSION: DEATH OR GLORY

Background

"All zones have now been opened and missiles unlocked. You're about to face a massive alien assault with low probability of survival. Your only hope now lies in careful planning. The Orox base has been exposed with a marker beacon and may be targeted at any time; it will require three direct missile hits to destroy it. However, destroying the base is likely to trigger an all-out assault by Orox warriors, which we will only be able to withstand with massive base defenses. As more Orox will continually arrive, you must time your missile launch to perfection. Too soon and we will have no base defenses, too late and we will face overwhelming force."

Main Objectives

- Destroy the Orox base.
- Kill all Orox warriors.

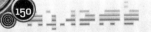

New Operatives

None

New Enemies

Orox Base

New Military Hardware

Commando Post

The Walkthrough

If you've gotten this far, you should be well down the road of *Space Colony* mastery. So we're going to be succinct and focus on the main points of strategy. In any case, this mission is very straightforward—nothing too tricky about it. You just have to blow up an enemy base and then kill five super-powerful Orox. Easy!

5-18. Run your Commandos away from their fragile posts to engage the Orox warriors.

Here's what to do:

- ☞ Pause the game. Sell off everything you can sell without jeopardizing your colonists' health and sanity. Sell all base defense structures—robot posts, lasers, hover mines, force field equipment, cluster bombs, even your Sentinel Posts, if you have any. We're going to take the fight to the enemy, or die trying.

- ☞ Target the Orox Base in the northeast corner of the map with all three of your Missile Silos. Click the Normal speed button and watch your missiles decimate the Orox Base. Check out your mission objective icon in the upper-left corner. Halfway done already!

- ☞ But now comes the hard part. Buy as many of the new Commando Posts as you can afford, placing them at least one length of the screen west of the Orox base. You want to run your fast Commandos from there to the Orox, keeping their posts out of the fray. Posts are very easy to destroy, especially by an Orox warrior. Remember, if a military robot's post is destroyed, the robot simply disappears. So don't needlessly endanger your troops by placing their posts in range of Orox blasts.

- ☞ In the unlikely event that you bought your full complement of 12 Commandos and still have more than 6000 credits left over, you have a choice. You can save the credits for replacement Commandos if you lose some in the upcoming battle. Or you can buy a Sentinel Post or two and place them next to your Commando Posts.

- ☞ Attack! Run your Commandos within range of an Orox warrior. If all 12 Commandos can concentrate fire on one Orox, the enemy will go down pretty quickly. Move from Orox to Orox, trying to keep all of your guns focused on one target at a time for maximum kill speed.

- Keep your workers mining and fabricating electronics back at the base. You may need the income for replacing destroyed Commandos or throwing in a few Hover Mine Delivery Systems if you're somewhat short of 6000 credits and the raging battle seems pretty even. A few mines might tip the scales in your favor!

- Tip: Pause frequently and check each of your Commando's health bars. If you have a Commando with health dropping into the red range, select only him and then click the "Send Selected Units Back to Posts" button (see 5-19). If you have a repair droid nearby, let him fix the Commando. Otherwise, just sell off the Commando for its depreciated cost and buy a new one. (Damaged Commandos don't lose any extra worth just because they're damaged!) This way you can get something out of the deal, instead of just losing the Commando completely to the next Orox blast.

- Keep hammering away! If your Commando ranks get too thin, pull back and sell off the survivors by clicking the "Sell Base Structures" cursor on their posts. The Orox will take their sweet time lumbering to your base; they have to stop and wail and destroy every puny human-built Light they pass on the way. This delay gives you time to build up more income so you can field the biggest possible squad of Commandos in your second wave of fighters.

- Once the last Orox falls, victory is yours.

5-20. Down go the Orox!

APPENDIX A
ROMANCE IN SPACE COLONY

Yes, romance is possible in space. Just like on Earth, dating in *Space Colony* can lead to that special friendship. But also like on Earth, certain pairings have a more realistic chance of success than others. Slim would leap through flaming hoops and bark like a seal for Venus if she asked him. On the other hand, Nailer has very little chance of getting Daisy to accompany him on a date of any kind.

The following tables list the chances that each colonist will say 'yes' to the any of the seven dating/romance questions posed by any of the other colonists. Note that these are base percentages. The actual percent chance listed in the game can be somewhat higher or lower depending on a number of factors too complex and mind numbing to enumerate here. Let's just say that the happier that both parties are, the better the chance that a date proposal will be accepted.

Important: Romance is more than just a sideshow of *Space Colony* gameplay. Colonists in love experience total Happiness for a period of time following the establishment of their "Special Friend" status. Thus, they work with great vigor and endurance for a while, giving your colony economy a healthy boost.

Special thanks to Sajjad Majid, Executive Producer of *Space Colony* at Gathering, for putting together these tables for us.

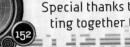

ROMANCE STATS

VENUS JONES BEING ASKED...

Asked by:	Let's go eat?	Want to get a drink?	Shall we dance?	Let's work out.	Come to the Sauna?	Dip in the Jacuzzi?	Will you be mine?	Time
Venus	0	0	0	0	0	0	0	0
Stig	40	80	70	40	30	50	50	96
Tami	40	50	30	30	30	30	20	72
Slim	30	50	40	30	30	40	40	96
Dean	50	80	70	40	50	60	60	96
Candy	40	80	50	30	30	30	20	72
Billy Bob	40	80	70	40	30	50	40	96
Nikolai	30	70	50	30	30	40	40	96
Daisy	40	80	30	30	30	30	20	72
Charles	40	80	70	40	30	50	40	96
Vasilios	40	80	70	40	30	50	40	96
Hoshi	40	80	30	30	30	40	20	72
Kita	40	80	30	30	30	40	20	72
Mr. Zhang	40	80	70	40	30	50	40	96
Greg	40	50	50	30	30	30	40	96
Babette	40	40	30	30	30	30	20	72
Nailer	20	50	30	30	20	20	20	96
Ashia	40	80	70	40	30	30	20	72
Bhoomi	40	80	70	40	30	30	20	72
Barbara	20	30	20	10	20	20	10	24

STIG SVENNSSON BEING ASKED...

Asked by:	Let's go eat?	Want to get a drink?	Shall we dance?	Let's work out.	Come to the Sauna?	Dip in the Jacuzzi?	Will you be mine?	Time
Venus	30	90	40	70	90	60	50	96
Stig	0	0	0	0	0	0	0	0
Tami	30	50	40	40	90	30	40	96
Slim	30	90	30	50	40	20	10	96
Dean	30	90	20	40	40	20	10	96
Candy	30	90	40	70	90	60	50	96
Billy Bob	30	90	20	50	40	20	10	96
Nikolai	30	90	20	50	40	20	10	96
Daisy	30	90	40	70	90	60	50	96
Charles	30	90	20	50	90	20	10	96
Vasilios	30	90	20	50	40	20	0	96
Hoshi	30	90	40	70	90	60	50	96
Kita	30	90	40	70	90	60	50	96
Mr. Zhang	30	90	20	70	40	10	10	96
Greg	30	50	40	50	90	40	20	96
Babette	30	90	40	70	90	60	50	48
Nailer	30	90	20	70	40	10	10	96
Ashia	30	90	40	70	90	60	50	96
Bhoomi	30	80	30	40	90	60	40	96
Barbara	30	50	30	40	70	30	30	96

TAMI BEING ASKED...

Asked by:	Let's go eat?	Want to get a drink?	Shall we dance?	Let's work out.	Come to the Sauna?	Dip in the Jacuzzi?	Will you be mine?	Time
Venus	30	95	40	10	40	40	30	48
Stig	30	85	50	0	40	40	40	48
Tami	0	0	0	0	0	0	0	0
Slim	20	95	60	10	50	50	60	48
Dean	30	95	70	30	50	50	70	60
Candy	30	95	40	10	40	40	30	48
Billy Bob	30	95	60	10	50	50	40	48
Nikolai	30	60	30	0	30	30	30	48
Daisy	30	95	60	10	30	30	30	48
Charles	30	95	60	10	50	50	60	48
Vasilios	30	95	60	10	50	50	30	48
Hoshi	20	60	20	0	20	20	20	48
Kita	20	60	20	0	20	20	20	48
Mr. Zhang	30	90	50	0	40	40	50	48
Greg	40	100	60	10	50	50	70	48
Babette	30	95	40	10	40	40	30	48
Nailer	50	100	70	10	50	50	60	120
Ashia	30	95	40	10	40	40	30	48
Bhoomi	30	95	40	10	40	40	10	48
Barbara	30	95	40	10	40	40	10	48

SLIM BEING ASKED...

Asked by:	Let's go eat?	Want to get a drink?	Shall we dance?	Let's work out.	Come to the Sauna?	Dip in the Jacuzzi?	Will you be mine?	Time
Venus	100	100	100	100	100	100	90	12
Stig	60	70	50	30	20	20	20	40
Tami	50	50	50	50	50	50	60	72
Slim	0	0	0	0	0	0	0	0
Dean	60	70	50	50	20	20	20	40
Candy	100	100	100	100	100	100	100	24
Billy Bob	50	50	50	30	20	20	10	40
Nikolai	60	70	50	50	20	20	20	40
Daisy	90	90	90	90	90	90	70	24
Charles	60	70	50	50	20	20	20	40
Vasilios	60	70	50	50	20	20	0	24
Hoshi	90	90	90	90	90	90	70	12
Kita	90	90	90	90	90	90	70	12
Mr. Zhang	60	70	50	50	20	20	20	40
Greg	60	70	50	50	20	20	20	40
Babette	100	100	100	100	100	100	90	24
Nailer	60	70	50	90	20	20	10	40
Ashia	90	90	90	90	90	90	80	24
Bhoomi	30	30	30	30	40	40	10	24
Barbara	80	80	80	80	80	80	60	24

DEAN BEING ASKED...

Asked by:	Let's go eat?	Want to get a drink?	Shall we dance?	Let's work out.	Come to the Sauna?	Dip in the Jacuzzi?	Will you be mine?	Time
Venus	70	10	40	70	70	70	60	120
Stig	60	0	20	40	20	20	20	24
Tami	50	0	30	50	50	50	40	96
Slim	60	0	20	40	20	20	20	24
Dean	0	0	0	0	0	0	0	0
Candy	60	0	30	60	60	60	50	96
Billy Bob	50	0	20	40	20	20	20	24
Nikolai	60	0	20	40	20	20	20	24
Daisy	60	0	30	60	60	60	50	96
Charles	60	0	20	40	20	20	20	24
Vasilios	60	0	20	40	20	20	0	24
Hoshi	60	0	30	60	60	60	50	96
Kita	60	0	30	60	60	60	50	96
Mr. Zhang	60	0	20	40	20	20	20	24
Greg	60	0	20	40	20	20	20	24
Babette	60	0	30	60	60	60	50	96
Nailer	30	0	20	20	20	20	20	24
Ashia	80	10	50	90	70	70	60	120
Bhoomi	60	0	30	60	50	50	40	96
Barbara	40	0	30	40	40	40	40	96

CANDY BEING ASKED...

Asked by:	Let's go eat?	Want to get a drink?	Shall we dance?	Let's work out.	Come to the Sauna?	Dip in the Jacuzzi?	Will you be mine?	Time
Venus	50	60	50	40	40	40	20	72
Stig	50	80	70	60	60	60	50	72
Tami	50	80	40	30	30	30	20	72
Slim	50	80	70	60	60	60	50	72
Dean	50	80	70	60	60	60	50	72
Candy	0	0	0	0	0	0	0	0
Billy Bob	50	80	70	60	60	60	50	72
Nikolai	50	80	70	60	60	60	50	72
Daisy	50	80	70	40	40	40	20	72
Charles	50	80	70	60	60	60	50	72
Vasilios	50	80	70	60	60	60	30	72
Hoshi	50	80	40	30	30	30	20	72
Kita	50	80	40	30	30	30	20	72
Mr. Zhang	50	80	70	60	50	50	40	72
Greg	50	80	70	60	60	60	50	72
Babette	50	80	70	40	30	30	20	72
Nailer	50	80	70	60	60	60	50	72
Ashia	50	60	50	40	40	40	20	72
Bhoomi	50	80	50	40	40	40	20	72
Barbara	50	80	50	40	40	40	20	72

BILLY BOB BEING ASKED...

Asked by:	Let's go eat?	Want to get a drink?	Shall we dance?	Let's work out.	Come to the Sauna?	Dip in the Jacuzzi?	Will you be mine?	Time
Venus	100	60	70	50	50	50	60	120
Stig	100	20	20	20	20	20	20	60
Tami	100	60	70	30	40	40	60	120
Slim	100	20	20	20	20	20	20	60
Dean	100	20	20	20	20	20	20	60
Candy	100	40	70	40	40	40	60	120
Billy Bob	0	0	0	0	0	0	0	0
Nikolai	100	20	20	20	20	20	20	60
Daisy	100	40	70	40	40	40	60	120
Charles	100	20	20	20	20	20	20	60
Vasilios	100	20	20	20	20	20	0	120
Hoshi	100	40	70	40	40	40	60	120
Kita	100	40	70	40	40	40	60	120
Mr. Zhang	100	20	20	20	20	20	20	60
Greg	100	20	20	20	20	20	20	60
Babette	100	40	70	40	40	40	60	120
Nailer	100	40	70	40	40	40	60	120
Ashia	100	40	70	40	40	40	60	120
Bhoomi	100	40	70	40	40	40	60	120
Barbara	100	40	70	40	40	40	60	120

NIKOLAI BEING ASKED...

Asked by:	Let's go eat?	Want to get a drink?	Shall we dance?	Let's work out.	Come to the Sauna?	Dip in the Jacuzzi?	Will you be mine?	Time
Venus	70	50	70	30	40	50	70	48
Stig	30	10	20	20	20	20	30	48
Tami	60	50	60	30	40	50	50	24
Slim	30	10	20	20	20	20	30	48
Dean	30	10	20	20	20	20	30	48
Candy	70	50	70	30	40	50	70	48
Billy Bob	30	10	20	20	20	20	30	48
Nikolai	0	0	0	0	0	0	0	0
Daisy	70	50	70	30	40	50	70	48
Charles	30	10	20	20	20	20	30	48
Vasilios	30	10	20	20	20	20	0	48
Hoshi	70	50	70	30	40	50	70	48
Kita	70	50	70	30	40	50	70	48
Mr. Zhang	30	10	20	20	20	20	30	48
Greg	30	10	20	20	20	20	30	48
Babette	70	50	70	30	40	50	70	48
Nailer	30	10	20	20	20	20	20	48
Ashia	70	50	70	30	40	50	60	48
Bhoomi	70	50	70	30	40	50	50	48
Barbara	70	50	70	30	40	50	70	48

DAISY BEING ASKED...

Asked by:	Let's go eat?	Want to get a drink?	Shall we dance?	Let's work out.	Come to the Sauna?	Dip in the Jacuzzi?	Will you be mine?	Time
Venus	20	40	50	20	40	30	40	120
Stig	20	40	50	30	60	50	40	120
Tami	20	60	50	30	40	20	30	72
Slim	20	40	50	30	50	40	30	60
Dean	30	70	60	30	60	50	50	120
Candy	20	40	50	30	40	30	30	120
Billy Bob	20	60	60	30	60	50	40	120
Nikolai	20	60	60	30	60	40	40	120
Daisy	0	0	0	0	0	0	0	0
Charles	20	60	60	30	60	50	40	120
Vasilios	20	60	60	30	60	50	40	120
Hoshi	20	40	60	20	30	30	30	120
Kita	20	40	60	20	30	30	30	120
Mr. Zhang	20	60	60	30	60	50	40	120
Greg	20	40	40	30	40	40	40	24
Babette	20	40	50	20	40	30	30	120
Nailer	20	40	50	20	40	40	20	60
Ashia	20	40	50	20	40	30	40	120
Bhoomi	20	40	60	20	40	30	40	120
Barbara	20	40	40	30	20	20	10	120

CHARLES BEING ASKED...

Asked by:	Let's go eat?	Want to get a drink?	Shall we dance?	Let's work out.	Come to the Sauna?	Dip in the Jacuzzi?	Will you be mine?	Time
Venus	60	80	70	50	70	70	70	72
Stig	60	80	40	20	30	30	30	72
Tami	70	90	80	50	70	70	70	60
Slim	50	70	40	20	30	30	30	48
Dean	50	70	40	20	30	30	30	40
Candy	60	80	70	50	70	70	70	72
Billy Bob	60	80	40	20	30	30	30	72
Nikolai	40	60	40	20	30	20	20	72
Daisy	60	80	70	50	70	70	70	72
Charles	0	0	0	0	0	0	0	0
Vasilios	60	80	40	20	30	30	0	72
Hoshi	60	80	70	50	70	70	60	72
Kita	60	80	70	50	70	70	60	72
Mr. Zhang	60	80	40	20	30	30	30	72
Greg	60	80	40	20	30	30	30	72
Babette	80	80	70	60	70	70	80	72
Nailer	30	40	10	10	10	10	10	72
Ashia	60	80	70	50	50	50	50	72
Bhoomi	60	80	70	50	70	70	70	120
Barbara	60	80	70	50	70	70	70	72

VASILIOS BEING ASKED...

Asked by:	Let's go eat?	Want to get a drink?	Shall we dance?	Let's work out.	Come to the Sauna?	Dip in the Jacuzzi?	Will you be mine?	Time
Venus	60	60	60	60	60	60	60	72
Stig	60	60	60	60	60	60	30	72
Tami	60	60	60	60	60	60	60	72
Slim	60	60	60	60	60	60	30	72
Dean	60	60	60	60	60	60	30	72
Candy	60	60	60	60	60	60	60	72
Billy Bob	60	60	60	60	60	60	30	72
Nikolai	60	60	60	60	60	60	30	72
Daisy	60	60	60	60	60	60	60	72
Charles	60	60	60	60	60	60	30	72
Vasilios	0	0	0	0	0	0	0	0
Hoshi	60	60	60	60	60	60	60	72
Kita	60	60	60	60	60	60	60	72
Mr. Zhang	60	60	60	60	60	60	30	72
Greg	60	60	60	60	60	60	30	72
Babette	60	60	60	60	60	60	60	72
Nailer	60	60	60	60	60	60	30	72
Ashia	60	60	60	60	60	60	60	72
Bhoomi	60	60	60	60	60	60	60	72
Barbara	60	60	60	60	60	60	60	72

HOSHI BEING ASKED...

Asked by:	Let's go eat?	Want to get a drink?	Shall we dance?	Let's work out.	Come to the Sauna?	Dip in the Jacuzzi?	Will you be mine?	Time
Venus	40	20	80	30	20	50	30	48
Stig	40	40	80	30	30	70	40	48
Tami	20	10	80	10	10	40	20	48
Slim	40	40	80	30	30	70	50	48
Dean	40	40	80	30	30	70	40	48
Candy	40	20	80	20	20	50	20	48
Billy Bob	40	40	80	30	30	70	40	48
Nikolai	40	40	80	30	30	70	30	48
Daisy	40	20	80	30	20	40	20	48
Charles	40	40	50	30	30	50	30	48
Vasilios	40	40	80	30	30	70	40	48
Hoshi	0	0	0	0	0	0	0	0
Kita	40	60	100	20	20	70	30	48
Mr. Zhang	40	40	80	30	30	40	20	48
Greg	40	40	80	30	30	70	40	48
Babette	40	40	80	20	20	20	20	48
Nailer	40	40	80	30	30	70	40	48
Ashia	40	40	80	20	20	20	20	48
Bhoomi	40	40	80	20	20	20	20	48
Barbara	40	40	80	20	20	20	20	48

KITA BEING ASKED...

Asked by:	Let's go eat?	Want to get a drink?	Shall we dance?	Let's work out.	Come to the Sauna?	Dip in the Jacuzzi?	Will you be mine?	Time
Venus	40	20	80	30	20	50	30	48
Stig	40	40	80	30	30	70	40	48
Tami	20	10	80	10	10	40	20	48
Slim	40	40	80	30	30	70	50	48
Dean	40	40	80	30	30	70	40	48
Candy	40	20	80	20	20	50	20	48
Billy Bob	40	40	80	30	30	70	40	48
Nikolai	40	40	80	30	30	70	30	48
Daisy	40	20	80	30	20	40	20	48
Charles	40	40	50	30	30	50	30	48
Vasilios	40	40	80	30	30	70	40	48
Hoshi	40	60	100	20	20	70	30	48
Kita	0	0	0	0	0	0	0	0
Mr. Zhang	40	40	80	30	30	40	20	48
Greg	40	40	80	30	30	70	40	48
Babette	40	40	80	20	20	20	20	48
Nailer	40	40	80	30	30	70	40	48
Ashia	40	40	80	20	20	20	20	48
Bhoomi	40	40	80	20	20	20	20	48
Barbara	40	40	80	20	20	20	20	48

MR. ZHANG BEING ASKED...

Asked by:	Let's go eat?	Want to get a drink?	Shall we dance?	Let's work out.	Come to the Sauna?	Dip in the Jacuzzi?	Will you be mine?	Time
Venus	50	80	60	80	60	60	60	96
Stig	30	40	20	40	20	20	20	24
Tami	50	60	60	80	60	60	50	96
Slim	30	40	20	40	20	20	20	24
Dean	30	40	20	40	20	20	20	24
Candy	50	60	60	80	60	60	50	96
Billy Bob	30	40	20	40	20	20	20	24
Nikolai	50	60	20	20	20	20	0	24
Daisy	50	60	60	80	60	60	50	96
Charles	30	40	20	40	20	20	20	24
Vasilios	30	40	20	40	20	20	0	24
Hoshi	50	60	60	80	60	60	40	96
Kita	50	60	60	80	60	60	40	96
Mr. Zhang	0	0	0	0	0	0	0	0
Greg	30	40	20	40	20	20	20	24
Babette	50	60	60	80	60	60	50	96
Nailer	30	40	20	40	20	20	20	24
Ashia	50	60	60	80	60	60	50	96
Bhoomi	50	60	60	80	60	60	60	120
Barbara	50	60	60	80	50	50	40	96

GREG BEING ASKED...

Asked by:	Let's go eat?	Want to get a drink?	Shall we dance?	Let's work out.	Come to the Sauna?	Dip in the Jacuzzi?	Will you be mine?	Time
Venus	90	90	90	90	90	100	70	36
Stig	20	40	20	20	20	20	20	72
Tami	60	60	60	60	60	70	50	48
Slim	20	40	20	20	20	20	20	72
Dean	20	40	20	20	20	20	20	72
Candy	90	90	90	90	90	100	70	48
Billy Bob	20	40	20	20	20	20	20	72
Nikolai	20	40	20	20	20	20	20	72
Daisy	80	80	80	80	80	100	60	48
Charles	20	40	20	20	20	20	20	72
Vasilios	20	40	20	20	20	20	0	72
Hoshi	80	80	80	80	80	100	60	48
Kita	80	80	80	80	80	100	60	48
Mr. Zhang	20	40	20	20	20	20	60	72
Greg	0	0	0	0	0	0	0	0
Babette	80	80	80	80	80	100	60	48
Nailer	20	40	20	20	20	20	20	72
Ashia	80	80	80	80	80	100	60	48
Bhoomi	60	60	60	60	60	50	30	48
Barbara	70	70	70	70	70	90	60	48

BABETTE BEING ASKED...

Asked by:	Let's go eat?	Want to get a drink?	Shall we dance?	Let's work out.	Come to the Sauna?	Dip in the Jacuzzi?	Will you be mine?	Time
Venus	30	40	30	10	30	30	30	72
Stig	40	60	50	40	50	50	40	72
Tami	20	30	20	10	20	30	30	72
Slim	40	60	50	40	50	50	40	72
Dean	40	60	60	50	50	50	50	72
Candy	30	40	30	10	30	30	30	72
Billy Bob	40	60	50	40	50	30	40	72
Nikolai	40	60	50	40	40	40	30	72
Daisy	30	40	30	10	30	30	30	72
Charles	40	60	50	40	50	50	40	72
Vasilios	40	60	50	40	50	50	20	72
Hoshi	30	40	30	10	30	30	30	72
Kita	30	40	30	10	30	30	30	72
Mr. Zhang	40	60	50	40	50	40	30	72
Greg	40	60	50	40	50	50	40	96
Babette	0	0	0	0	0	0	0	0
Nailer	40	60	50	40	50	50	40	72
Ashia	40	60	30	10	30	30	30	96
Bhoomi	40	60	30	10	30	30	30	72
Barbara	40	60	30	20	30	30	30	72

NAILER BEING ASKED...

Asked by:	Let's go eat?	Want to get a drink?	Shall we dance?	Let's work out.	Come to the Sauna?	Dip in the Jacuzzi?	Will you be mine?	Time
Venus	60	70	30	80	50	50	40	48
Stig	60	70	0	20	20	20	0	48
Tami	60	90	30	80	50	50	50	48
Slim	60	70	0	20	20	20	0	48
Dean	60	70	0	20	20	20	0	48
Candy	60	70	30	80	50	50	40	48
Billy Bob	60	70	0	20	20	20	0	48
Nikolai	60	70	0	20	20	20	0	48
Daisy	60	70	30	80	50	50	40	48
Charles	60	70	0	20	20	20	0	48
Vasilios	60	70	0	20	20	20	0	48
Hoshi	60	70	30	80	50	50	40	48
Kita	60	70	30	80	50	50	40	48
Mr. Zhang	60	70	0	20	20	20	0	48
Greg	60	70	0	20	20	20	0	48
Babette	60	70	30	80	50	50	40	48
Nailer	0	0	0	0	0	0	0	0
Ashia	60	70	30	80	50	50	40	48
Bhoomi	60	70	30	80	50	50	40	48
Barbara	60	70	30	80	50	50	40	48

ASHIA BEING ASKED...

Asked by:	Let's go eat?	Want to get a drink?	Shall we dance?	Let's work out.	Come to the Sauna?	Dip in the Jacuzzi?	Will you be mine?	Time
Venus	30	50	60	90	30	30	20	96
Stig	30	70	70	90	40	40	40	96
Tami	30	50	60	90	30	30	20	96
Slim	30	70	70	90	40	40	40	96
Dean	50	70	70	90	50	50	50	120
Candy	30	50	60	90	30	30	20	96
Billy Bob	30	70	70	90	40	40	40	96
Nikolai	30	70	70	90	40	40	30	96
Daisy	30	50	60	90	30	30	20	96
Charles	30	60	60	70	30	30	30	96
Vasilios	30	70	70	90	40	40	30	96
Hoshi	30	50	60	90	30	30	20	96
Kita	30	50	60	90	30	30	20	96
Mr. Zhang	30	70	70	90	40	40	30	96
Greg	30	60	60	70	40	40	30	48
Babette	30	50	60	90	30	30	20	96
Nailer	30	70	70	90	40	40	30	96
Ashia	0	0	0	0	0	0	0	0
Bhoomi	30	50	60	90	30	30	20	96
Barbara	30	30	40	60	30	30	10	96

BHOOMI BEING ASKED...

Asked by:	Let's go eat?	Want to get a drink?	Shall we dance?	Let's work out.	Come to the Sauna?	Dip in the Jacuzzi?	Will you be mine?	Time
Venus	70	20	40	40	20	20	20	60
Stig	70	20	40	40	60	50	40	120
Tami	70	20	40	40	20	20	20	60
Slim	70	20	40	40	60	50	30	120
Dean	70	20	40	40	60	50	40	120
Candy	70	20	40	40	20	20	20	60
Billy Bob	70	20	40	40	60	50	40	120
Nikolai	70	20	40	40	60	50	30	120
Daisy	70	20	40	40	20	20	20	60
Charles	70	20	40	40	60	50	40	120
Vasilios	70	20	40	40	60	50	40	120
Hoshi	70	20	40	40	20	20	20	60
Kita	70	20	40	40	20	20	20	60
Mr. Zhang	70	20	40	40	60	50	40	120
Greg	60	20	40	40	50	50	40	60
Babette	70	20	40	40	20	20	20	60
Nailer	60	20	40	40	50	50	30	120
Ashia	70	20	40	40	20	20	20	60
Bhoomi	0	0	0	0	0	0	0	0
Barbara	70	20	40	40	20	20	10	60

BARBARA BEING ASKED...

Asked by:	Let's go eat?	Want to get a drink?	Shall we dance?	Let's work out.	Come to the Sauna?	Dip in the Jacuzzi?	Will you be mine?	Time
Venus	30	60	30	30	30	30	40	72
Stig	30	80	50	50	60	60	50	72
Tami	30	60	30	30	30	30	30	72
Slim	30	80	50	50	60	60	40	72
Dean	30	80	50	50	60	60	60	72
Candy	30	80	30	30	30	30	30	72
Billy Bob	30	80	50	50	40	40	10	72
Nikolai	30	80	50	50	60	60	40	72
Daisy	30	80	30	30	30	30	40	72
Charles	30	80	50	50	60	60	60	72
Vasilios	30	80	50	50	50	50	20	72
Hoshi	30	80	30	30	30	30	40	72
Kita	30	80	30	30	30	30	40	72
Mr. Zhang	30	80	50	50	40	40	40	72
Greg	30	70	50	50	60	60	50	72
Babette	30	60	30	30	30	30	40	72
Nailer	30	80	50	50	60	60	50	72
Ashia	30	60	30	30	30	30	40	72
Bhoomi	30	50	30	30	30	30	20	72
Barbara	0	0	0	0	0	0	0	0

SPACE COLONY
OFFICIAL STRATEGY GUIDE

ISBN: 0-7440-0334-2

Library of Congress No.: 2003112408

Printing Code: The rightmost double-digit number is the year of the book's printing; the rightmost single-digit number is the number of the book's printing. For example, 03-1 shows that the first printing of the book occurred in 2003.

06 05 04 03   4 3 2 1

Manufactured in the United States of America.

BRADYGAMES STAFF

PUBLISHER
David Waybright

EDITOR-IN-CHIEF
H. Leigh Davis

MARKETING MANAGER
Janet Eshenour

CREATIVE DIRECTOR
Robin Lasek

LICENSING MANAGER
Mike Degler

ASSISTANT MARKETING MANAGER
Susie Nieman

CREDITS

SENIOR DEVELOPMENT EDITOR
David B. Bartley

SCREENSHOT EDITOR
Michael Owen

BOOK DESIGNER
Carol Stamile

PRODUCTION DESIGNER
Amy Hassos